The Hellenistic Mysteries

& Christianity

Unveiling deeper meanings of
Hellenistic and Gospel texts,
revealing a profound
cosmic reality.

Adrian Anderson   Ph.D.

Also available by this author:
The Rudolf Steiner Handbook
The Foundation Stone Meditation: a new commentary
The Way the Sacred
Living a Spiritual year: seasonal festivals

See also
Damien Pryor:

The Lalibela Handbook
The Great Pyramid and the Sphinx
The Externsteine: Europe's greatest Celtic site
Stonehenge: The essential guide to its purpose and context
The tropical zodiac, its origin and validity; the origin of the zodiac signs

Threshold Publishing Australia

ISBN 978-0-9941602-0-1

CONTENTS

CHAPTER ONE
Ancient Greece: a new epoch begins

Introduction
In this book we shall explore the main features of the Classical Greek spiritual wisdom and that of the later Hellenistic Age, with its famous Mysteries. Then we shall see how this relates to emergence of Christianity and the deeper esoteric significance of this religion. Underlying this exploration is the perspective on these subjects developed by Rudolf Steiner, but the reader will not need any knowledge of his works to enjoy this book. A useful guide and introduction to the ideas of Rudolf Steiner is contained this author's book, the Rudolf Steiner Handbook.

The spiritual views and practices of earlier cultures were quite different to those of the Grecian people, in that they still had specially designed sacred temples with secret chambers or alignments to celestial events. It is understood that all earlier cultures had a form of the Mysteries, or at least secret religious rites. In ancient Egypt and Sumeria, at the Externsteine and at some other places, the mystical-religious life developed to a complex and sophisticated level. The sites explored in the books by Damien Pryor are useful here. These books are about The Great Pyramid & the Sphinx, Stonehenge and associated British sites, the Externsteine in Germany, and Lalibela in Ethiopia.

Around 750 BC Classical Greek civilisation began to emerge as the leading cultural civilization in the lands around the shores of the Aegean and Mediterranean seas. Within a few centuries such was the cultural splendour that developed in Athens in many fields of higher creativity, that historians can speak of 'the Golden Age of Greece'. These fields included architecture, the visual arts and the performing arts, and social-political reforms (the city-states). It is well-known that this civilisation had a cultural feature known as the Mysteries.

The Mysteries is the name for religious procedures undertaken by temple institutions that were designed to achieve an interaction with the sacred; with the gods revered in their civilisation. As such the Mysteries offered both publicly accessible festivals and strictly secret initiatory rituals, wherein an experience of the spiritual could be provided. This means the spiritual both within the soul of the acolyte, and in the cosmos beyond the physical world.

1

Testimonials from notable people of the Greco-Latin world establish that many people considered that the Mysteries were a major reason, or even the major reason, for the cultural greatness of Athens. For example, Cicero, (orator, writer, noted civic official) from the 1st century BC, wrote in reference to the Eleusinian Mysteries,

> For it appears to me that among the many exceptional and divine things your Athens has produced and contributed to human life, nothing is better than those Mysteries. For by means of them we have been transported from a rough and savage way of life to the state of humanity, and have been civilized.[1]

But in contrast to these earlier cultures, the achievements that were taking Greece to new heights of cultural achievement, especially Athens, were striking testimonials to something new. Namely the active engagement of a more individualized type of activity in that society. For example, for the first time in history, when an artist made his sculpture, or pottery, etc, he now signed his artwork. [2]

By the Hellenistic Age the vast numbers of physical labourers toiling away at a stupendous task like the construction of Stonehenge, or the Great Pyramid, were gone. The buildings in these extraordinary sacred sites were designed to represent complex celestial rhythms of the stars, the sun and moon.

In the Hellenistic Age some splendid temples were erected in the honour of Diana, or other deities. But these no longer reflected celestial rhythms in their architecture, nor were they constructed from colossal stone blocks, and in circumstances where even today, it would be bordering on the impossible to achieve the task.

Changing attitudes to the spiritual and the after-life
In ancient Greece the most gifted creative people longed to be publicly acknowledged as a master of their art, either at the Olympic Games or at a cultural festivals. The artworks of the Greco-Latin era became testimonials to the personal creativity and spirituality of artisans who felt themselves to be

---

[1] The Ancient Mysteries, edit. Marvin W. Myer, Univ. Pennsylvania, Philadelphia, 1999.
[2] See any standard art history text, e.g., Gardner's Art through the Ages, the Western Perspective, Fred S Kleiner article *Greek vase painting*, Wadsworth/Cengage Learning.

individuals, and who sensed that they had to focus their own mind on their creative tasks, if they were to produce the desired result. This contrasts so strongly with earlier cultural attitudes, where anonymous artists carried out their tasks from the inspiration which they believed they received from their gods. These artisans and artists were required to assist in the building of a sacred site for the worship of their god.

These changes indicate that a much stronger sense of the personal self was arising in people in this era. In the preceding Mesopotamian-Egyptian Age, at least in its earlier phases, people did not have such an individuated sense of self, but instead they possessed a different quality. As Rudolf Steiner taught and as their artworks indicate, they had a sense of being immersed in a divine milieu in a living cosmos maintained actively by the gods. They possessed some kind of natural psychic sensitivity, which Rudolf Steiner calls the old clairvoyance.[3]

Another really incisive, if subtle, change in how human beings experienced themselves in those earlier ages is indicated in the fact that now, for the first time in history, a palpable fear of death arose, as a cultural phenomenon. Strange as it might sound, the world's first literary records of the fear of death, namely that death would lead to a terrible, meaningless existence, are found amongst the Greeks of the Classical Age. In all earlier writings, the belief in a meaningful, even joyous, after-life was self-evident, and a striking feature of these earlier peoples. But all this changed by the time the ancient Greek civilisation was developing.

This new fear amongst the Greeks of the Classical Age is indicated for example in Homer's *Odyssey*, where a deceased soul, summoned up from the Netherworld to speak with the hero Odysseus, says,

> "Speak not comfortably to me, renowned Odysseus, of death, for indeed would I rather be a penniless peasant farmer....than rule over an entire host of dissipating dead..."   (Song 11: lines 488-491)
> (Author's translation)

Another indication of this new attitude to the after-life as something terribly dreary and disempowered, is found in an

---

[3] See my book, Rudolf Steiner Handbook for more about this theme.

initiatory text, the Hymn to Demeter, which derives from the wonderful Mysteries of Eleusis,

> Blessed is he amongst earthly humans who has seen these things {of the Mysteries}, but he who dies without fulfilling the holy things, and he who has no share in them, he has no claim ever on such blessings when dead and departed to mouldy darkness..." [1]

In a drama called *Agamemnon*, written by the great Greek dramatist Aeschylos, the hero can overcome his fear of death to some extent when faced with a terrifying ordeal, but it is certainly not a welcome existence, because it is a kind of non-existence,

> "Would that some fate might come, speedily, not too-painfully, nor with lingering {sick-}bed, bringing us to everlasting, endless sleep." [4]   (lines 1448ff)

This new attitude contrasts strongly with the intense focus, and happy expectation in all earlier cultures on the after-life, with its promise of an existence amongst the gods. A strong belief in the after-life is the reason why, in earlier times there was such emphasis on religious or moral values, and why the rites for the deceased ancestors were so important. One's existence after death was a real one, but it could be either terrible or wonderful, depending upon one's conduct and the help obtained from special rites carried out for you by the living.

This entire attitude is poignantly expressed in the Egyptian Book of the Dead, from the early centuries of the Egyptian Old Kingdom, where the priests in their rites on behalf of the dead proclaim various affirmations. The deceased, now journeying in his soul, approaches the realm of the sun, which is the realm of the sun god Osiris, and says, via the priests who are reading the rites on his behalf,

Hail Lord, thou most mighty and awe-inspiring soul! Truly, I, even I, have come to gaze upon thee – do thou make me exalted! I have made my way through the Underworld and I have opened up paths of heaven...I have journeyed on and have reached those divine beings...the wardens of the Temple of Osiris ! Homage to ye, ye Lords of Kas ...ye who live in

---

[4] Aeschylos, *Agamemnon* trans. P. Vellacott, Penguin Classics 1956.

eternity, I have opened up a pathway for myself to you! [5]
(chapters 72, 73.)

In fact what we know as the Book of the Dead was actually called the Book of the Coming Forth by Day, such was the sense of radiance attached to existence in the soul realms in those remote times. But in Egypt too, as the Hellenistic age dawned, Egyptian people like those of Greece, began to lament about and to fear the disempowered, murky realm in which the dead are forced to exist. A funeral text from Egypt, dated to 64 BC, speaks of this,

> "...The West (the realm of the dead) is a land of slumber, dark and heavy, the habitation of those yonder, sleeping in their mummies, not waking to perceive their brethren, nor noticing their mothers and fathers... [6]

It is well-known that in earlier cultures, there was an emphasis upon the after-life, and hence on the reality of the gods and spirit realms, and consequently no fear of death, in the more modern sense. But this very significant point that in Greek literature we find the first specific indications of the fear of death, needs to be understood in a balanced way. Certainly in remote ages all people, including the Greeks, had a fear of a painful death, or of murder, but not of death itself, which was thought of as a kind of gateway into spiritual realms.

People of earlier ages felt that they could, if they lived a moral life, journey onwards and upwards to the radiant realm of the sun god. As the old holistic or psychic consciousness died away, then a fear arose, for people began to feel that they were living in a bare, empty physical reality, without any spiritual realms behind it. And as a natural part of this change was a gradual development of a disbelief in the conviction of their ancestors about spirit realms. These became just a figment of the imagination, and gradually the rites for the dead ceased in many places. The age-old holistic sensing, which used to allow the everyday environment to be permeated by a subtle spiritual ambience, was fading out.

Furthermore, materialism now emerged as a specifically thought-out basis for a scientific world-view. It was the Greek thinkers, Leucippos and his student Democritos who for the

---

[5] The Book of the Dead, trans. E. A. Wallis-Budge, RKP London, 1969.
[6] Hastings Encyclopaedia of Religion and Ethics, vol. 8, p.22, 1915 edition.

first time in history, began to regard creation, at its most fundamental level, as consisting only of very tiny particles of matter, which he termed 'atoms'. To these ancient Greeks the 'atoms' were not as small or as complex as the atoms in our modern meaning of this term. However, previously there had been an attitude that the origin of matter was in a realm more subtle than matter. A realm composed of ethereal energies, referred to as the 'four elements', sometimes including a subtle energy referred to as the 'aether'.

These dramatic differences between the earlier cultures and the now dawning classical Grecian age tells us that the times were changing, and the ancient natural belief in spirit and subtle energies was dying out. An individualized way of encountering the world was emerging, and the kind of expanded psychic-holistic consciousness that created the ancient sacred sites, was now fading away.

A memorable testimonial to this epochal sea-change in humanity's consciousness – that of the rise of materialism – is to be found in a Hellenistic Hebrew text, from about 100 BC, called the Wisdom of Solomon. In this the writer laments the rise of materialism, indirectly quoting people who in his lifetime were developing a view which expressed doubt about the existence of the soul and the after-life:

> But…godless people…said to themselves, in their deluded way … "When a person dies, there is no solution {to death}, no one was ever known who returned from the grave. By mere chance were we born …. our body turns to ashes, and the breath of life will disperse like empty air" ….. But as a child…a noble soul fell to my lot; or, rather, I myself was noble, and {so} I entered into an unblemished body…
> (The *Wisdom of Solomon*, The New English Bible)

In other words, the writer witnesses with dismay the birth of a new attitude of materialism which views the soul as a by-product of nerve and brain processes, and regards the after-life as a fantasy, born of yearning for survival. Whereas by contrast, he himself accepts the idea of reincarnation, or at least, of an existence before conception, in spirit realms.

No more huge initiatory temple complexes
In the new era of the Greco-Latin Age, as compared to ancient Egypt and Babylonia, etc, we are not going to encounter sacred sites made possible by the use of a formidable holistic-psychic

capacity, enabling people to construct buildings or monuments which embody complex cosmic dynamics. The sacred sites will be much less striking. For the Golden Age of Greece is not an era which produced great sacred sites of formidable engineering complexity, in response to complex astronomical alignments, like those of the Giza plateau, or at Stonehenge.

The earlier sacred sites, with their almost impossibly accurate alignments, and complex structures mirroring the cosmos, would never again appear. Instead, brilliantly gifted, individualized people would produce the varied cultural richness of the new Hellenistic age. There were still sacred sites, dedicated to the quest for spirituality, now called "the Mysteries", but these were different to the older sacred sites. Their buildings were devoid of secret chambers, with no correspondence to star patterns or symbiotic harmony with natural features of the landscape. And these institutions now existed within a culture where there was a growing class of people for whom the spiritual quest was not so important.

Another striking sign of this change, of this evolving of consciousness, is the fact that philosophy arose for the first time in history, in this Grecian Age. Here we need to distinguish the word 'philosophy' from the word, 'mysticism', which is the psychic beholding of realities not of the physical world, and then contemplating what they might mean. Historically, philosophical contemplations were at first really mystical pursuits. This is illustrated by a passage in Plato's "Republic" where the pursuit of 'philosophy' is said to greatly assist in determining the nature of one's next incarnation (whether human or animal, etc).[7] But gradually, 'philosophy' became the application of rigorous logical analysis to ever less spiritual themes.

The mystic may certainly work out his or her ideas about spiritual beings or cosmic mysteries, but these spiritual thoughts came into consciousness in the first place via some initiatory process, or through mystical visions. Whereas by contrast, the philosopher applies rigorous analysis to ideas about questions which need not be seen in a spiritual light, such as the nature of consciousness, e.g., our capacity to cognize things. But these philosophical mental exertions require no prior mystical visions, nor input from any spiritual experience or esoteric doctrines.

---

[7] From Book 10, paragraph 619 e.

This is what the term philosophy has come to mean to us; so it is not really correct to call the ancient mystics or sages, 'philosophers'. Although the ancients did use this term for mystics, but in an era when it still meant a love of spiritual insightfulness, or holistic wisdom.

Philosophy in the intellectual, non-mystical form arose especially through the efforts of the famous ancient Greek thinker, Aristotle. The incisiveness of Aristotle's analysis of consciousness, and of life-questions in general was so potent, that single-handedly he created the new science of logic, which has become designated as 'philosophy'. The philosophical process of logic, its analysis of ideas, is quite distinct from experiencing mystical insights, for these flow by themselves into the mind.

But, as Rudolf Steiner points out, the wisdom of an Egyptian or Celtic or Neolithic priest, or of the great Grecian mystics like Pythagoras or Heraclitos, was something that they were given 'from above', it was something which they intuitively experienced or psychically saw. They did not have to strenuously work it out in the intellect.

One gets the impression, indeed it is quite clearly stated in various of the esoteric texts of this Age, that such people felt that divine beings were letting these truths descend into their soul. Some texts speak of how the mystic even directly experienced encounters with such beings. This brief look at philosophy versus mysticism gives a clue to what is happening in the Greek Age with regards to sacred sites and the quest for spirituality.

There is now the emergence of philosophy as the individualized quest for clarity about questions of human nature, etc, through logical analysis in one's own mind. This change is to be seen in the differences in the world-view of Plato – the great mystic – and that of Aristotle, the great philosopher. Plato was also a capable logical thinker, and Aristotle as a young man, had shown an interest in mystical teachings. Plato possessed knowledge about many deeper spiritual themes, and discussed spirit realms and various qualities inherent to the soul. A good example of this is his doctrine of the Realm of the Archetypal Idea.

In this realm of the Idea there exists, according to Plato, the 'concept' of all things; it is rather like 'the mind of God' which formed the idea of the realms of nature, and then created them as reality. This is really inferring a realm that is far removed from the physical sphere, and also far beyond the common idea of a soul realm, as found in the beliefs and religions of many earlier cultures. For in the realm of souls are to be found the souls of the dead, and those souls who are awaiting birth (or re-birth), together with spiritual beings.

But Plato's realm of the Idea is far beyond this, it is much more transcendent; it is a realm in which the archetypal forms of all things exist. But Plato did not obtain these ideas from logical deduction, they were mystical insights of his own soul, or were communicated to him from esoteric sources.

Plato and Aristotle
It is believed by many people that Plato was initiated into the Mysteries of Eleusis; Rudolf Steiner taught that this was in fact the case. There is no historical proof of this, but one gains this impression from various comments found in his works. For example, in his Symposium, he mentions 'the lesser mysteries (of love)' and then he refers to 'greater and more hidden mysteries'. Such phrases can be seen as indirect reference to the Mysteries, because the terms, Lesser and greater Mysteries were specifically used about the Mysteries of Eleusis. The Lesser Mysteries took place in early spring, and the Greater Mysteries took place in the autumn, and occupied nine days. [8] Another work of his, *Phaedrus,* has passages so transcendent that the origin is very likely to be from the Mysteries. For example, this occurs in his *Phaedrus*;

> But all souls do not easily recall the things of the other world; they may have seen them for a short time only, or they may have been unfortunate in their earthly lot, and, having had their hearts turned to unrighteousness through some corrupting influence, they may have lost the memory of the holy things which once they saw.
> (translated B. Jowett)

One can of course conclude that such a perspective is obtained either from initiation in the Mysteries, or from his own spiritual contemplation. The same two possibilities can be said in regard

[8] See J. Reif, The Mysteries of Demeter, Weiser, 2000 / The Hutchinson Encyclopaedia (http://encyclopaedia.farlex.com/Eleusinian+Mysteries /http://www.arthistory.sbc.edu/imageswomen

to another passage in his Phaedo. He refers to the fate of the soul in the after-life, as taught in the Mysteries, namely as either a descent into the dreary Underworld after death, but for the initiate, an ascent to blessed realms.

> And I conceive that the founders of the Mysteries had a real meaning and were not mere triflers when they intimated in a figure long ago that he who passes unsanctified and uninitiated into the Underworld will live in a slough, but that he who arrives there after initiation and purification will dwell with the gods.
>
> (translated B. Jowett)

There is a subtle inference here that Plato speaks from inner knowledge of the Mysteries, not just hearsay, but yet it still does not constitute proof. In contrast to Plato himself, his famous student Aristotle did not make any references to the transcendent teachings of the Mysteries. He restricted himself primarily to those ideas from the Mysteries that could be subject to rigorous logical analysis.

One small reference to a specifically esoteric idea does survive, but from a much later source, and it is only presumed to be from Aristotle. It is about the Mysteries having their special power because they placed acolytes into a certain special frame of mind, rather than teaching specifics. And also Aristotles' treatise called *Categories* can be seen as inherently, even if indirectly, mystical.[9]

However, Aristotle, as a forerunner to the humanists, rejected Plato's theory of an archetypal 'realm of Ideas', and also his affirmation of reincarnation, because logical assessment of these did not appear to support their underlying implications. As a young man, Aristotle had studied under Plato for twenty years; but as a mature man, he went his own way, and after Plato's death, he developed a non-mystical, highly analytical worldview, encompassing all fields of knowledge, to a level of detail and clarity which was without equal.

There is no evidence of Aristotle ever having been initiated into the Mysteries, although he once took a student of his, the young Alexander the Great, to the Mystery centre at Samothrace. There

---

[9] There is an apparently genuine letter from Alexander the Great to Aristotle, reprimanding him because he allowed his private lectures to be published. But in fact these were probably of a challenging philosophical nature, not really of an 'esoteric' or mystical kind.

at Samothrace, according to Rudolf Steiner, Aristotle had some peripheral involvement with its Mysteries, which were of significance to his inner life. But this occurred in a more subtle manner, for unlike the mystics of his time, Aristotle never promoted nor emphasized the Mysteries, nor acknowledged any indebtedness to them.

Aristotle argued against Plato's doctrine of the Archetypal Idea, saying that these supposed 'archetypal ideas' certainly could not exist as realities in their own right, separated from the physical things that they represent. Here is the essence of a new, non-holistic attitude which was arising in this Age, and which now permeates the modern world. A teacher in the old Mysteries would respond to Aristotle's criticism by saying that no matter how sharp is one's logic, it can never convincingly disprove (nor for that matter, prove) the reality of a spiritual realm, for its window on the world sees logical thought, not transcendent spiritual things. But Aristotle was not concerned with objections from the Mysteries, his task was to develop the power of individualized logical thinking.

And Plato's realm of the Idea is an especially spiritual one; its Ideas are the origin of all created things. It is a realm where divine spirit beings interweave their creative intentions with the necessities of humanity, living in a realm far below, in matter.

This point that logical thinking which gradually has become materialistic cannot 'see' such realities, is beautifully presented by the great German writer, Johann Wolfgang von Goethe (1747-1832), in his drama, Faust. Dr. Faust is a bored humanist, who feels that there must be more to life than what intellectual knowledge offers, so he goes off on a search for this greater something, with the help of a strange spirit being.

In Part Two, this sinister spirit being, Mephistopheles, who represents disbelief in the spiritual quest (amongst other things), tries to dissuade Faust, who has now entered the after-death realms, from going into this remote archetypal realm of Plato. He tries to persuade Faust that such a realm does not really exist, or if it does, it consists of nothingness; he tells Faust,

> And if you had swum through the ocean,
> and there beheld boundless space,
> You would nevertheless see wave upon wave coming;
> even though you might be afraid of going under,

You would at least see something!
Perhaps dolphins streaking by in the greenness of stilled seas,
see perhaps also clouds floating past, see sun, moon and stars –
Nothing shall you see in the eternally empty distance,
Neither hear your own footstep, nor find
any solid thing, whereupon you may rest!
Descend then! I could say – arise! .....
Flee from the Created to the realm freed of structured forms!
Be delighted amidst what long since has ceased to be!
(trans. by author) [10]

Faust famously answers him, "In your 'nothing' I hope to find the All!" The point here is that to the person who is restricted to purely logical analysis, spirit realms (or even subtle ethereal energies) are beyond their mental horizon. These things cannot have any place in their worldview.

But the realm of the Idea was a truth to those in the Mysteries. It was a realm where structured forms, made of matter, don't exist. Rather the 'idea' of all formed things exist there – and these are living images, formed and sustained in the consciousness of spirit beings. This includes the idea of things which once existed, long ago. What then were the key Mystery Centres or spiritual thinkers of the Hellenistic world?

---

[10] Johann Wolfgang von Goethe, Faust, Part Two, ls. 6240-6245, 6275-78, Hamburger edition, Vol. 3, E. Trunz, Edit. Christian Wegner Verlag, Hamburg, 1949.

CHAPTER TWO The Greek Mystery centres

The spirituality of the Mysteries

What were the ancient Grecian Mysteries? How did they nurture the quest for spirituality in that Age? We can begin exploring this many-facetted theme, by considering a brief but profound sentence (an epigram) which shows deep insight into the spiritual aspect of life. It embodies the attitude of people who attained initiation into the Greek Mysteries. The origin of the thousands of such epigrams is often unknown, but some people have concluded that this one comes from Plato. It is a striking sentence that affirms that we human beings have a higher self, and that it is like a star shining above one's soul.

The epigram also suggests that the stars in the heavens are not limited just to their physical appearance, but they are also spiritual beings. This same attitude is found in the earlier Babylonian literature, where the term for 'star' and for 'spirit-being' is almost the same thing. For example in the Babylonian story of the Deluge (their version of the Biblical Flood and the Epic of Gilgamesh) the text refers to 'star-gods'. So Plato's sentence is this:

> Thou gazest to distant stars, my star; would that I were heaven, so that I may look at thee with {my} many eyes!
> [11]   (author's translation)

In other words, the mystic's higher spiritual-self (his star) turns its gaze up to the star-beings of the heavens, and Plato wishes that he were the starry heaven itself. He says in a more precise rendering of the Greek, "would that I had been created as heaven", {i.e., not created as a human}. Then he, being the starry heaven itself, could look down upon this glorious, spiritual part of the human being, with all of his 'eyes', that is with all of the stars (star-beings) in the firmament. In fact, so sophisticated is the ancient Greek language, that Plato can use a beautiful, poetic word for the 'eye' (ommaso), for which there is no equivalent in modern languages.[12]

---

[11] In E. Irwin, Colour terms in Greek poetry, Hakkert, Toronto, 1974 p.105

[12] Plato's Greek: ἀστέρας εἰσαθρεῖς ἀστήρ ἐμὸς · εἴθε γενοίμην οὐρανός ὡς πολλοῖς ὄμμασω εἰς σέ βλέπω. The verb translated by me as 'gaze to ... distant (stars)' literally says that the star "descries the stars" which means, it looks at stars that are in the distance. The linking of this sentence to Plato, and then to a male associate of Plato, is speculation.

Rudolf Steiner taught that the acolytes in antiquity who entered into the process offered by the Mysteries sought to have a direct encounter with the divine, and to thereby unite with their higher self. Steiner points out that a key part of the process involved a type of 'sleep' that lasted for three-days. During this time the acolyte was released from the body, and would come to know the mysterious soul world, where spiritual beings, and the souls of the dead, exist.

The soul world was called the Underworld, referring to the fact that in this process they would experience cosmic forces operative in the human soul but which lie beneath normal consciousness; they are in the subconscious. This was also the realm of those who have died. At some point in the training the acolyte, once out of their body, would ascend into a higher realm to encounter a sacred being, often the sun god.

So, if such wonderful mystical insights as these came from the Mysteries of Greece, where were their sacred sites, and what was their main focus? We won't be examining in detail the history and mythology of these sites, instead we shall focus on getting clarity about the over-all situation, and how the advent of Christianity changed this, and how secretly there is a link between the Mysteries and the events in the life of Christ.

Athens
What is today the capital city of Greece, was in ancient times the city-state of Athens, and it was here that the Golden Age of Greece occurred. Although it is not itself a Mystery Centre site, its magnificent temple, the Parthenon, was sacred to the goddess Pallas Athena. It is known that this goddess became equated by the Greeks with the Egyptian goddess Isis, and yet somehow she was also viewed as a goddess of war, but also represented the intellectual side of justice. To add further confusion, she was regarded as a 'virginal goddess'.

Rudolf Steiner is able to provide an understanding of Pallas Athena that brings clarity to these various attributes. He explains that Pallas Athena was perceived by those in the Mysteries as the inspirer of wisdom, and therefore similar to the Egyptian goddess Isis. But Steiner empathized that it was a case in the Hellenistic Age of a wisdom which was gained by engaging in the material world, even if it was looked upon as the realm of illusion, not by shunning it.

Thus she represents those forces which, after the loss of the age-old clairvoyance, (a loss that was perceptible to the Hellenistic people), made possible an individualized, wisdom-filled world-view. But this enlightenment was only possible to those who entered the Mysteries. The understanding of life attained in this way is deeply spiritual. Through this kind of consciousness, the human being was saved from a complete separation from the cosmos.

This is also why Pallas Athena is considered virginal; the wisdom she provided to the seeker after initiation was developed by the seeker from within, it was not grafted on to them by an external influence. Consequently the helmet which is usually depicted on her head, actually had nothing to do with war. The configuration around her head indicates the energies of cosmic wisdom, weaving around her head. And her shielding cape with a gorgon on it, indicates that those who develop the inner wisdom that Athena assists one to achieve, have conquered the lower self.

Pallas Athena is also known as Athena "Tritogeneia"[13]. This term has remained a riddle to scholars, and to the ancient Greeks. One theory is that it means 'born of the triton', but since 'tri' means 'three', most theories factor in the term 'three'; such as 'born on the third day'. However I conclude that what was considered by the ancient Greeks to be the literal meaning of the term, 'thrice-born', is the correct meaning. So this epithet for the goddess means the spiritual wisdom born of the threefold soul, composed as it is of the three faculties of thinking, feeling and will.

Delphi

A brief look at the Delphic oracle site, and some writings from Plutarch, an initiated priest of Delphi, who wrote about AD 100, gives us some idea of the spirituality of the ancient Grecian Mysteries. The striking landscape around Delphi, on the southern slopes of Mt. Parnassos, and near to the cliffs of the Phaedriades, was sacred to Apollo, and to the Muses, and also to a lesser extent, Dionysos. The worship of Apollo appears to have commenced there about 700 BC. The steep mountain cliffs and natural beauty of the area still evokes a potent feeling of the sacred in the visitor today.

---

[13] In Greek, τρῑτογένεια.

This became the most famous oracle site in the world; the oracle would seat herself in the modest temple, set amongst the fissures and rocks, and give voice to remarkable prophecies and advice. Athletic contests, called the Pythian Games, were staged here very four years, to celebrate the victory of Apollo over an evil serpent. But it appears that in the very early time of this site, musical contests were held every eight years.

Another indicator of the wisdom prevailing here is the sculpture of a sphinx, the Naxian Sphinx, which was discovered in 1861. This sphinx, a human head placed on a composite animal body, like all the sphinxes found in ancient Greek sites, symbolizes the imperfect self, the so-called lower self. The famous 'dark night of the soul' of medieval mystics derives from their encounter with this shadow-side of the human being. As some Greek legends indicate, when the acolyte strives towards the divine, this part of the personality rises up and demands to be conquered before any access is given to the sacred realms.

In his treatise on Isis and Osiris, the venerable high priest of Delphi, Plutarch, writes about the guiding principles of the spirituality surrounding the quest for the Mysteries. Speaking to a younger person in this essay, he says,

> It is necessary O Klea, that people of intelligence entreat the gods for all things good – especially understanding of the gods, in so far as this is accessible to human beings…..for the human being can not receive anything greater, nor can the Gods bestow upon them anything more ennobling, than the truth…. The longing for truth is the same as the longing for Divinity – especially that longing for truth which is seeking the truth of the Gods. This is like acquiring a comprehension of the Sacred, like having a search for real purity and it is like the holy rituals to the gods performed in the temple. [14]
>
> (translated the author)

Here is a profound and noble teaching, indeed the ethics expressed here are not at all contrary to the values of the much later Christian religion, which in the 5th and 6th centuries forcibly closed down the Mysteries. We shall be examining a hymn to

---

[14] Greek text in "Plutarch über Isis und Osiris" edit. Gustav Parthey, Berlin Nicolaische Buchhandlung, 1850, p. 2,3.

Apollo later on, and discover just how transcendent and inspirational was the wisdom of the priesthood of Apollo.

Eleusis

A major part of the Mysteries of ancient Greece were those of Eleusis, a sacred site not far from Athens, where the Mysteries connected with the myth of Demeter, Persephone and Pluto was the focus. Today all that is left are the poignant ruins of the temple complex, near an uninspiring industrial area. The actual content of the core Mystery rites of Eleusis remains unknown, however some of the activity involved included a procession, ritual bathing in the sea, and beholding of various sacred objects.

These procedures occurred against the background of the myth about Persephone. This myth tells how Demeter's daughter, Persephone, was carried off against her will by Pluto down into the underworld. She eventually regained her freedom through the intervention of Zeus, but still has to disappear down into Pluto's realm for four months of each year.

The esoteric interpretation of this myth was never made public; indeed the teachings of the Mysteries were kept secret, under pain of death. But a small number of indirect comments about Eleusis are known. The famous Roman orator Cicero praised the Eleusinian Mysteries, saying that,

> "We have learned from {these rites} about the beginnings of life, and we have gained the power not only to live happily, but also to die with better hope..." [15]

This indicates not only an enhanced ethics and optimism was given to the acolytes, but they also knew about the after-life and how to meet the reality of being mortal with tranquillity. This is in fact a much more significant statement than is often realized, considering how the people in the Hellenistic world were now facing a fear of death. We shall return to this when exploring the secrets of the new religion of this era, Christianity.

Rudolf Steiner taught that Demeter was understood as the divine creator of the eternal spirit in the human being, but that she was also viewed as the clairvoyant, enlightened

---

[15] In De Legibus, in The Mysteries, papers from the Eranos Yearbooks, edit. J. Campbell, Vol. 2, Bollingen Series XXX Princeton Uni. Press, 1990, p. 349.

17

consciousness of the spiritual teacher. Pluto was then to the Greeks the power, in material substances, that diminished the spiritual consciousness. And in a broader sense, Demeter was representative of the same divine tapestry of energies which originally created the Earth.[16]

Samothrace

Another major Mystery centre was on Samothrace, a windswept island in the northern Aegean Sea, its rugged countryside is dominated by a high mountain, Mt. Phengari. The ruins of the sacred initiation temple can be seen today on the north coast of the island, overlooking the sea. The floor and various columns of the great hall (the Anaktoron) are still standing. This centre was established prior to Greek settlers arriving there, but it is regarded as part of the Grecian Mysteries. The actual nature of the initiatory experience here, like that of Eleusis, was kept secret, but some details of a ritual procession and requirements for admission did become known.

Here deities referred to as 'the Cabiri' (or Kabeiroi) were venerated; the nature of these beings remains unclear to scholars, but a Cabiren vase dating from the fourth century BC depicts, amongst other figures, an ugly dwarf-like being whose name is Pratolaos. This term appears to mean something like, 'the first or earliest generation of the human being'. Rudolf Steiner taught that these deities are linked to the primordial spiritual origin of the human being, and of the Earth. This teaching is supported by archaeological excavation on Samothrace which has revealed evidence of the worship of the Cybele. This goddess is an ancient form of the earth-mother.

It is quite likely that the ancient historian Herodotus is correct when he writes that these Mysteries derive from the indigenous people on this island, and were gratefully assimilated by the Greeks. Rudolf Steiner indicates that the spiritual focus of the people here involved a deep contemplation of the higher-self's influence in us (something like the conscience) and its battle against the lower earthly self, which was seen as supported by flesh-based pleasures and urges. This conclusion seems likely from the few indications about the Samothracian Mysteries that have survived. These report that the priests there demanded

---

[16] His lecture cycle of August 1911 in Munch discusses this, "Wonders of the world , trials of the soul and revelations of the spirit".

18

from enquirers that they make a kind of confession about any unethical deeds that they have made.[17]

Ephesus

Another significant site was established by the Greeks on the coast of Asia Minor (present day Turkey), at Ephesus, where a great temple, called the Artemision. It was built to honour the goddess Artemis, who was regarded as a chaste goddess, and a goddess of birth (amongst other things). She was known as "Diana" to the Romans. Later in the Imperial Age of the Roman Empire, Artemis was equated with various goddesses, and in particular, as a goddess of the moon, hence she was associated with the Egyptian goddess Isis. The temple was magnificent; a Greek mathematician, Philon, writing ca. 150 BC records that he had seen ...

> "..the wonders of the ancient world...the walls and hanging gardens of old Babylon, the mighty work of the high pyramids, the lighthouse of Pharos, the Colossus of Rhodes, and the tomb of Mausolus. But when I saw the temple of Ephesus, rising to the clouds, all these wonders were put into the shade." [18]

Of course Philon, writing long after access to the interior of the Great Pyramid was sealed off was not aware of the sheer genius underlying the construction of this building, nor of its esoteric significance. But from what we know of the dimensions of the temple, and the beauty of classical Grecian architecture, this mood of wonder at the Ephesian temple's obvious beauty and size is understandable. We know more about the temple than we do about the significance of the goddess Artemis.

But her functions became intertwined with a variety of features belonging to nature and fertility goddesses across the Mediterranean world; these other deities are associated with fertility rites, and wild untamed elements of nature. Unlike the sacred sites of earlier Ages, with their astronomical alignments or symbolic structures, the features of the temple of Ephesus do not indicate symbolically the spiritual focus of its cult. The actual esoteric focus of the Mysteries at Ephesus eludes all scholarly research.

---

[17] The Mysteries of the Kabeiroi, in The Mysteries, Papers from the Eranos Yearbooks, edit. Joseph Campbell, Bollingen Paperbacks, Princeton 1978.
[18] E. Pepper & J. Wilcock, Magical and Mystical sites, Abacus, London, 1978, p. 22.

But Rudolf Steiner taught that at this centre, the enigma of how creation merges into the physical world, out of the ether, but ultimately from spiritual realms, was researched. For example, the riddle of how the soul descended down to birth via the moon sphere, and how nature spirits animated and maintained physical life. This process they personified and called Persephone.[19]

Pythagoras

Another significant place for the spiritual quest in this Age was a small settlement established by the famous sage Pythagoras in lower Italy, in Croton (or Crotona), present-day Crotone. Pythagoras (ca. 580 BC - 490 BC) was originally from the Greek town of Samos, but he began a travel program that took him specifically to sacred sites, including the most important Egyptian town for the cult of the sun god; Heliopolis, the primary sacred site of the Sun Mysteries. A primary initiatory aim in the Sun Mysteries was to ascend up to the sun god Ra in one's disembodied soul. Here too, according to Plato, ancient records of Egypt from pre-historical ages were carefully preserved.

Pythagoras is reported to have stayed here for 22 years; and after the Persians invaded Egypt, he was taken to Persia, where he stayed for 12 years. At 56 years of age, he established his centre for initiatory striving in Croton, and the influence of his many students caused the town to become the leading town culturally amongst the Achaean towns in Italy. Pythagoras taught that the life-style one leads has to be adapted to the requirements of spiritual striving, such as adopting vegetarianism.

His students could be either men or women, both sexes were treated as equals. Acolytes were required to pass severe ordeals of courage and integrity, and then they could enter an initiatory process which lasted from two to five years. Pythagoras became known as the wisest of sages, and it was said that the famous oracle at Delphi predicted his birth.

He travelled widely, to sacred sites in Egypt and elsewhere, gathering experience and learning. He taught the pre-existence of the soul, and reincarnation, and how the soul needs to find

---

[19] His lecture cycle of August 1911 in Munch discusses this, "Wonders of the world , trials of the soul and revelations of the spirit".

20

its way out of the limitations imposed upon consciousness by existence in the flesh body.

He expounded on the role and importance of music as an expression of a sacred geometry, linked to the cosmos. In other words, he discovered the mathematical basis of the intervals in the musical scale. Plato was in many respects a follower of Pythagoras, and he taught that music has a soul-quality to it, that music should uplift and ennoble the soul.

Plato and Pythagoras saw a link between music and the subtle energies of the planets, orbiting around us in their heavenly spheres, that is, the seven-octave scale is a reflection of energies in the seven planets. There were a number of other strands to the sacred sites of the Greco-Latin Age, such as a small settlement at the town of Elis, founded in the 5th century BC, by Phaeton, a follower of Socrates; we shall refer to this centre a little later. And Hermias, ruler of Atarneus, encouraged some of Plato's leading students to found a new mystical school at the town of Assos.

Now, in noting the existence of such centres as that at Croton, Assos and Elis, we are also discovering that the great sacred sites of previous ages, which were the primary focus of communities of people in the surrounding region, have given way to small communal settlements. Many of these based were on the initiative of one individual, who gradually developed a personal following, and probably had a modest temple.

In addition to these centres, there were many branches of the various cults which had spread across the entire Mediterranean world. This included the rites of Isis, of Mithra, of Seraphis, of Adonis, of Cybele, and of course the well-known Greek gods, such as Apollo, Jupiter, Zeus, and others.

But as the teachings of these Mystery religions or cults were kept confidential, there is little that can be said about the nature of specific Mysteries. There are a few guarded comments in various Hellenistic writers, but there exist two tantalising, powerful revelations from the Hellenistic Age about initiation, we shall consider these soon.

Additionally, in modern times, there are invaluable comments and explanations on some of these from Rudolf Steiner. However in the literature from this Age, there are also many impressive mystical texts that must have their origins in the Mysteries of this Age. They show a deep, inspiring spirituality.

One of the two very revealing statements is attributed to a Greek writer named Themistios from about 350 AD, when the Mysteries were losing their authority and power,

> The soul at death has the same experience as those who are being initiated into the Great Mysteries... at first one wanders and wearily hurries to and fro, and journeys with suspicion through the dark, as if not initiated. Then come all the terrors, before the final initiation shuddering, trembling, amazement.

> Then one is impacted by a marvellous light, and one is received into pure regions and meadows, with voices and dances and the majesty of holy sounds and shapes. Being amongst these, he who has fulfilled initiation wanders free, released and bearing his crown, joins in the divine communion, and consorts with pure and holy men.[20]

The second statement comes in a 2nd century AD novel about the spiritual path and the goddess Isis, called The Golden Ass of Apuleius.

The Grecian Mysteries of Isis

The Egyptian Mysteries of Isis lived on in this Age amongst the Hellenistic peoples, and a valuable glimpse into their esoteric world view is given in the collection of esoteric Greek texts called Corpus Hermeticum. Here we shall just note that in these texts, a profoundly esoteric, deeply insightful view of the cosmos is given. One experiences a multi-level universe, inhabited by many different kinds of spirit beings, both of planetary and zodiacal nature. However, as the basis of the esoteric knowledge in these texts derives from ancient Egyptian Mysteries, we won't go into the details of it here.

Rudolf Steiner indicates that in the earlier Egyptian Mysteries, the understanding and experiences of Isis were deeper than those obtained in the Hellenistic experiences. To the ancient Egyptians she was a kind of personification of the creators of the human being. She was one of various divine beings, whom

---

[20] Published in Themistius: on Aristotle On the Soul; R.Todd (trans.) Bristol Classic Press 1996.

the initiate experienced as the origin of his or her own innermost spiritual nature.

But a glimpse into the core initiatory experiences of an acolyte in the Hellenistic Isis Mysteries is to be found in a famous text called "The Golden Ass" written by Apuleius, a Roman citizen from Morocco, who lived in the 2nd century AD. This is a fictional account of a man's adventures, culminating in initiation in these rites. Towards the end is a brief but potent description of the initiatory experience. It is perhaps the single most revealing description in Hellenistic literature of the great forbidden theme, namely what took place in the initiatory rites of the Mysteries:

> I approached the very gates of death and set one foot upon Proserpine's threshold, yet was permitted to return, enraptured, through all the elements...I entered the presence of the gods of the Under-world and the gods of the Upper-world, stood near them and worshipped them. [21]

We see again, as with the ancient Egyptian Book of the Dead, that a successful journey across the threshold into the murky Hades realms, and then up into radiant realms, is the crucial thing to achieve. From such experiences as these, it is clear that a considerable body of knowledge about the spiritual realities would have accumulated over centuries.

The Neo-Platonists
Though much of this mystical wisdom was kept confidential, many discussions and brief exploratory texts were inspired by it, and this resulted in detailed mystical views on the deeper questions of life becoming public knowledge. These were bound to be codified, and written down eventually; this is in effect what the writings of Plato are.

Then 600 years later, in the early centuries of the Christian era, many other texts appeared, in which the general impact of Plato and of other persons with initiatory knowledge, were written down and compared; these became the Neo-Platonists writings. One of the most important neo-Platonists in the early centuries

---

[21] Apuleius, The Golden Ass, trans. Robert Graves, Harmondsworth: Penguin, 1956 p. 286.

23

of the Christian era was Porphyry, a pupil of Plotinos, who was perhaps the foremost neo-Platonist.

Plotinus and Porphyry stand out as very capable representatives of the Mystery teachings and doctrines of Plato, as understood in the twilight years of the Greek civilization. We won't examine the teachings of the neo-Platonists in detail, who lived early in the Christian era. But we shall note one important text from Porphyry, which in our translation reveals a striking spiritual-mystical perspective. This text from Porphyry is found in his commentary of some passages in Homer, so we need to consider some passages from the great writings of the immortal Homer, who wrote in the 8th century BC.

His two great writings are The Iliad and The Odyssey. The first is a story of adventure and heroism against the background of the Trojan War. But the second text, the Odyssey, is quite different. In the guise of an adventure story about Odysseus, it conveys discreetly many of the secrets of the process of being initiated.

CHAPTER THREE The initiation wisdom of Homer

Homer's Odyssey Book 13

Homer's great epic written about 750 BC, is commonly regarded as a story of adventures and challenges experienced by Odyssey, a Greek warrior. But this is a very incomplete view; for hidden in the text there is an esoteric theme, presenting the process of initiation. The Odyssey is written in a complex and multi-nuanced Greek, and is one of the greatest literary achievements in history. It has been associated with today's social idea of 'initiation', meaning the need of young males to be guided through specific stages of the maturation process.

It has also been seen as an initiatory narrative in the deeper original sense of the word, by a few mystically inclined people in the western world. Rudolf Steiner specifically defined Homer as an initiate, and his book, the Odyssey, as an account of initiation, of the search for the eternal higher ego. It is then in fact an allegorical narrative of the way to initiation or spiritualization. To clarify his statements, Steiner gave a translation of the Prologue of the Odyssey. But his version differs widely from the accepted versions.

A typical translation, from German, Dutch, French or English academics, goes like this, in English,[22]

> Tell me, O muse, of the man who travelled far and wide after he attacked the holy citadel of Troy. He saw the cities of many people and he learnt of their customs. He suffered much at sea while trying to **save** his own **life** and to bring his comrades home. But he failed to save his comrades in spite of all his efforts.

One needs to note here that some of the translations will say "save his soul" but 'save his life' is meant; the word 'soul' is used as a stand-in for the word 'life'. Here one concludes that the great epic is a story of masculine daring and courage, trying to stay alive against great odds. But Rudolf Steiner's version is this,

---

[22] I checked 14 translations, one in Dutch, two in French, the rest in German & English

Tell me, Muse, of the man, the one who journeyed so much, who wandered astray so much, since he destroyed holy Troy.
Many cities of people he saw, and many customs he learned.
And also who endured in pain, so much, in the sea of tormenting suffering,
striving for **his own soul** and for his friends' home-coming.

Here the prologue is announcing an initiatory quest to obtain one's own true soul, and in the process undergoing much inner suffering, within the symbolic sea of the soul. This reading of the prologue is very different. The editors of Rudolf Steiner's book in the official German Complete Works, simply point out that the academic translation, (as it were, the correct one), is quite different to Steiner's.[23]

But then the editors of two English translations of Steiner's book, published in 1947 and 1991 respectively, in view of the contradiction between Rudolf Steiner's version and all academic versions, went further. They decided to censor Steiner's version and replace it with the commonly accepted version.[24] (!) This meant that Steiner's assertion that it was an initiation book, which he stated before and also after his version of the prologue, became rather absurd, since the quote placed in the book does not establish this at all.

So what is the real situation here? The Odyssey is one of the greatest pieces of literature in the world, still evoking intense interest after nearly 3,000 years. Why is this? My conclusion is because, like Dante's Divine Comedy, veiled behind its striking imagery is the potent theme of becoming initiated. Nevertheless it still has great value when read at the level of an epic of male courage and decisiveness. I have carefully translated the prologue of this epic and found that Rudolf Steiner was precisely correct, and other translations of this passage are incorrect here. They don't take note of a subtle indication in the ancient Greek that the great epic is about the initiatory quest. Such translations ignore certain subtleties in Homer's Greek,

---

[23] In the German book the editors comment, this line in the Prologue actually literally says, '... in order to save his soul and the homecoming of his comrades.' (As we noted above, it is understood in all translations of the Odyssey, that where the translator put 'his soul', this means his **life**, as many versions say.)
[24] The 1947 version edited by O. Wannamaker and 1991, edited by Andrew Welburn.

which indicate an initiatory meaning is also being conveyed. Firstly, Homer does **not** say that Odysseus seeks to 'save' his life (nor 'rescue' nor 'preserve' it). Homer uses the verb 'arnumai' (ἄρνῡμαι) which means to **'win'** or to **'gain'**, and in so doing, gaining fame or honour. It does **not** mean to save. Further, Homer writes about the 'soul' which is to be gained, not simply his (physical) life as such.

So, Odysseus is on a quest to **gain** his own soul, a process which shall bring him, much honour or reward, if he is successful. This is indeed a very apt description of the initiatory quest. It is important in such passages to translate as closely as possible to the original.

For the original text reveals a veiled meaning if we can develop a discerning eye. To discover this deeper narrative, the text has to be more precisely translated, following the specific details in the original, at the expense of losing a nicely flowing epic 'feel'.

Secondly, I also note that the expression usually translated as, "on the sea" in terms of Attic Greek grammar, can be entirely accurately translated as "within the sea"; and this term symbolically used, means the Soul World. We note also that in his prologue Homer does not mention any boat at all, but later on boats are involved, but some are described as magical things.

Thirdly, I found that Homer does **not** refer to his hero as simply physically 'suffering'. He three times states that Odysseus suffers in regard to his soul-life, in regard to his desires and passions.

Consequently this Prologue is then correctly translated as follows, (I'm using a rather wordy style here to make the hidden meaning much clearer),

> Tell me, Muse, of the man, much travelled, who very much wandered-astray, since he attacked the sacred citadel of Troy. Many cities of people he saw, and customs he learnt. And also, within the {soul-}sea, many soul-pains he suffered in his feelings, throughout his passions, to attain <u>that</u> soul, and thereby *great honour*, and rescue his comrades. But none of the comrades did he rescue, however much he tried.

This passage when translated with awareness of the nuances from Homer's initiatory wisdom, reveal a different story. Lets see it now with key phrases in bold font,

> Tell me, Muse, of the man, much travelled, who very much wandered-astray, since he attacked the sacred citadel of Troy. Many cities of people he saw, and customs he learnt. And also, **within** the {soul-}sea, many **soul-pains** he suffered **in his feelings**, **throughout his passions**, to **attain** *that* soul, and thereby *great honour* and rescue his conrades. But none of his comrades did he rescue, however much he tried.

So in summary, what we have discovered, confirms Steiner's version. We note again that the verb 'to gain' or 'to attain' (his soul) is used, and not the verb to 'save'. And since this remarkable verb also means to gain much honour or praise in the attaining of one's goals, the insightful reader realizes that this is a veiled way of saying "initiation". For this verb lends itself to winning the Olympic Games or attaining to initiation – both brought honour and praise.

A further fact here is that the usual translations ignore the little word 'that' (in Greek: 'haen' / ἥν) which can sometimes be ignored in translating. You see above that I have emphasized this word, for in this text it is actually very important indeed. This word here emphasises that it is this same suffering soul that Odysseus is seeking to attain, but in its true, redeemed condition. (See the Appendix for a clear colour-coded presentation of my translation.)

We also saw that although in the surface meaning Odysseus was "at sea" (hence one naturally assumes in a boat), the Greek text does allow the other translation too, "within the sea" – meaning the sea of one's own emotionality. There are three specific references to emotional stress, and the references to distress are precisely about suffering in regard to the emotions, specifically to the desires. This puts emphasis on the desires, and hence on the basic requirement for the acolyte to undergo some purification, or catharsis. Homer literally says, "...suffered in his feelings, {this suffering} throughout his passions..."

So it is a very imperfect translation that condenses and blunts Homer's precise text into "He suffered much at sea..." along the lines of an adventure story at sea. For Odysseus is setting sail out into the ocean of his own emotional energies and lower desires. Behind this is his intention of **attaining** his higher soul or spiritual self. None of his companions shall get back home, because they are the lower qualities in his own soul that he needs to remove. So it is very reasonable to conclude that the Odyssey is an initiatory text, and that the epic story, at its deepest level, is about the struggles encountered in the quest for higher development, not about physical battles and trials.

This allows us now to understand another misunderstood core initiation text from the ancient Grecian world. In chapter 13 of the Odyssey, a significant aspect of the initiatory quest is indicated. This is where Odysseus returns to his homeland, Ithaca. In this chapter, the mysterious *cave of the nymphs* is described. About 1,100 years later, a Greek Neo-Platonist, Porphyry (233-305 AD) focussed on this episode and wrote a small treatise in which he interpreted the mystical statements from Homer about this cave. Porphyry's treatise on the passage in the Odyssey about the Cave of the Nymphs is important, but his interpretation is not always correct.

Again virtually all translations of the Odyssey are not useful here, as the text is translated without the insight needed to convey the initiatory secrets being presented. All academic translators, so far as I can see, are unaware that here in the passage about the cave of the nymphs, and in the prologue, and throughout the entire book, there is a hidden meaning. The 18th century scholar, Thomas Taylor, was aware of this mystical meaning, but his translation suffers from a subjective approach, which causes him to change the actual Greek text. He also uses a very florid style, and of course his English is centuries out of date. So let's now unveil the meaning the Cave of the Nymphs.

The Cave of the Nymphs
In Book Thirteen, Odysseus is brought back to a cave on Ithaca, fast asleep; this island is where he was born. This happens against the background of the good gods striving to help him attain his higher soul, against the assaults of malignant beings of all kinds. There follows a famous passage about the features of this mysterious cave. But since it is the birthplace of the hero, this episode is in effect symbolizing the physical world, or indeed, the process of incarnating into the physical world. It becomes clear as we read this passage in Greek, that numerous mystical statements are packed into a small paragraph, involving many esoteric themes.

Let's see how the usual translation goes,

> At the head of this harbour there is a large olive tree,
> and at no great distance a fine overarching cavern
> sacred to the nymphs who are called Naiads.
> There are mixing bowls within it and wine-jars of stone
> and the bees hive there.
> Moreover, there are great looms of stone
> on which the nymphs weave their robes of sea purple
> -- very curious to see -- and at all times
> there is water within it. It has two entrances,
> one facing North by which mortals can go down into the cave,
> while the other comes from the South
> and is more mysterious; mortals cannot possibly get in by it,
> it is the way taken by the gods.

There are many errors or unhelpful nuances in this translation. Firstly, the olive tree is not a 'large' one; this is a false translation. In Homer's Greek it is actually called a 'long-leaved' tree. But it is not so helpful to use this term in the translation, or to translate it as 'shady' or very large, etc. The adjective 'long-leaved' has an important meaning in the ancient world of Homer, nearly 3,000 years ago.

Very many species of olive trees have been developed in recent times, so that at least 260 species are now fruit-bearing, whether their leaves are short or long. But in ancient Greece, wild undeveloped species were very common, but cultivated ones were less common than today. The wild olive trees had smaller leaves and smaller fruit than the cultivated longer-leaved olive trees; the latter produce better olives.[25]

Secondly, the usual translations may refer to the cave itself as 'sinister and delightful' (!) or just as 'fine'. But the Greek word for 'sinister' also means shady, misty or dim; and this is what is implied here. The usual version, coupling sinister with delightful, is illogical. So it is a misty and delightful cave. By now we become aware that the cave represents the mineral-physical body, and that we humans experience it as delightful, even though it is a dim place compared with the our true home in spirit realms.

---

[25] Sophai Rhizopoulou, American-Eurasian J. Agric. & Environ. Sci, 2 (4) *Olea Europaea L. A Botanical Contribution To Culture*, ps 282-387 2007.

Then there is the strange reference to bees, as in the above academic version, "and the bees hive there". But in this phrase, there is also a Greek word epeita (ἔπειτα) which can provide emphasis to what is being said. So it requires a word like 'moreover' (or 'also') to be present in a translation. In this passage some emphasis is certainly needed. But many translators leave out this emphasizing word, saying; 'bees lay up stores of honey' or ' bees hive there'. But let's just note that the text is saying that inside a misty cavern there is storing up of honey (i.e., in effect, bee-hives). This is of course a completely unnatural situation !

Here is a strong spiritual metaphor, for bees do not have hives in dim moist caves! So this hint therefore needs emphasis. We shall see what the reference to bees really means later. And now to another section with a faulty translation. It is said that the nymphs "weave their robes of **sea purple**", and indeed this is literally what the Greek term says. But what does that mean, if anything at all? For 'sea-purple' means nothing to modern readers. The correct translation here, but only in the first instance, is 'true purple', "they weave their robes of **true purple**". The situation is that in ancient Greece a colour which approximates to our purple was often obtained from lichen or roots of some plants.

However the best colour was obtained by crushing the small Murex mollusc, whose glands released an intense purplish colour. (10,000 of these were needed to dye one woollen toga.) So, the expression, 'sea-purple' simply refers to the superior intensity of the colour. But now another fact has to be considered; the colour produced from the mollusc was actually a brighter, redder form of purple, more correctly defined as **crimson**. [26] So, Homer was saying that the nymphs **are weaving cloth of crimson**; we shall examine the significance this statement later. Now let's read the passage again, but in my translation where I have tried to give this wonderful initiatory text its correct nuance,

> Moreover at the head of this harbour is an olive tree, capable of fruit-bearing; and near to this, {is} a cave – misty and delightful – sacred to the nymphs known as the Naiades.

---

[26] This crimson mollusk secretion is known as Tyrian purple (Oxf.Dict / http://core.edu.edu/psyc).

And in this (cave) are mixing bowls and amphorae, of
stone.
And moreover there wild bees store honey.
In it (the cave) are tall marble looms, for there nymphs
weave cloth, of crimson – a wonder to behold.
And water flows unceasingly in this cave.
And two openings it has. By the one to the north,
humans descend.
The one to the south is divine, men do not enter by that
place, at all. Rather it is (an opening for) the path for
immortals.

Interpreting the passage

At the head of the harbour
The cave itself represents the physical-material plane, for the
entire passage is about the nature of the physical world into
which the incarnating soul descends. As Porphyry mentions, in
Greek mythology the goddess Athene was born from the head
of Zeus, and Athene created the olive tree herself. So, in the
language of the initiatory myth, Odysseus is now approaching a
phase of the initiatory quest wherein this goddess can help him
**gain an understanding of the process of entry into the
material world, into flesh, by human souls**.

The process of spiritual enlightenment requires that one gains
some understanding of just how the process of entering into life
on Earth affects our spiritual potential. The cave is our physical
body See below for the reason why the olives are important.

A fruit-bearing olive tree
As we noted above, it is not that the olive-tree is especially
shady, rather it bears good, full fruits. So we can ask now, what
is symbolized by a cave with an olive-bearing tree nearby? The
answer is, our body, in which we live and through which we
have our earthly experience that we absorb.

A person living in the material world absorbs life-experiences –
and it is according to Rudolf Steiner a chief characteristic of the
olives that they especially strongly absorb terrestrial life-forces
(etheric energies arising from the soil). The life-experiences
which we human beings absorb, become in effect, our harvest;
what we distil from all of the experiences we undergo. Just as
the people in the Mediterranean lands distilled the valuable
olive oil from the olive fruit.

misty and delightful
The material world is somewhat dark, compared to a realm consisting only of spiritual light. And yet it is experienced as delightful, for a major attitude in the ancient Mystery wisdom is that incarnating souls generally feel the prospect of life again in the flesh as very alluring, because of the earthly pleasures it offers. And furthermore, ancient traditions and medieval folklore assert that the influence of the undines or Naiades is an especially attractive one to the adult human being, as eroticism derives from these beings. It is precisely the dominance of these energies which the acolyte like Odysseus has to overcome.

sacred to nymphs
Or one could also translate this as, 'dedicated to nymphs'. This indicates that the nymphs need a moist environment in order to be active, and their activity involves forming the flesh-watery human body.

mixing bowls and amphorae of stone
The mention of these two items indicates that the 'cave' is a place where the nymphs combine various elemental energies and then connect these to matter, a process that assists the embryo to form.

wild bees
This is an intriguing statement ! It is known that in various ancient religions high spiritual activity is associated with bees. The reason for this is that the activity of the bee, in gathering nectar from flowers which has been formed by the sunlight's actions, and then metamorphosing this into honey, is a good parallel to the process of spiritualization, which is closely associated with 'the spiritual sun' in the Mysteries.

The acolyte was to gather up the experiences offered from their interaction with the temple and its initiatory process, and metamorphose this into wisdom and goodness. The process of incarnating could also be viewed as a process in which 'Everyman' gathers up life experiences, which metamorphose into higher soul qualities over the course of lifetimes.

tall looms
The translation 'tall looms' is a better rendering than 'huge looms'. If the looms are described as being in the vertical plane (tall), and the Greek word does mean this, then they represent the skeletal system of the human being, around which the flesh is woven. So, the choice of 'tall' esoterically indicates the hard

minerals of our skeleton which are **in the vertical plane**, rather than in the horizontal plane. The intention of Homer was not to indicate that these 'looms' are of huge size.

Nymphs weave cloth
The meaning here is that the water sprites (called Naiades in Greece, or in medieval folklore, undines) are important, their energies were involved in the forming of protoplasm, this includes the cells of the flesh body. And flesh is in fact primarily made of water (about 80%). The next phrase clarifies this.

crimson
The colour of the 'cloth' is much better described as crimson than as sea-purple, because crimson **refers to the colour of flesh and blood**.

A wonder to behold
We realize that this statement is exaggerated with regard to cloth, but it is quite appropriate for the marvel of the human body.

Water flows unceasingly
In the real physical world this would mean springs, but the cave is not a physical reality; so the reference is to a life-force which continually pervades the Earth.

And two openings it has
These two openings or interfaces refer to the descending into matter by incarnating souls, and on the other hand, the ascent up out of the material world.

The one in the north is for humans
The north was, to the ancient Greeks, in the direction of coldness and hardening; the hardening of water into ice. Hence the north represents the hardening process whereby an immaterial being takes on a material body. So the north stands for incarnating.

The southern opening is divine
This indicates that in the south is the interface with the higher worlds, the spiritual realms. The south, to the ancient Greeks, being in the direction of the equatorial zone, it represents heat and thusly, a vaporizing or de-materializing process.

Men do not enter the place at all.
The point here appears to be that incarnating people do not come in by this opening or interface, precisely because incarnating or descending is only possible by the other opening. This one, in the south, then is for human beings who are passing away from the physical world and arising into spirit realms, so to speak.

Rather it is the path for immortals
The word 'immortals' in Greek literature can refer to gods, but as Porphyry says, it is can also refer to human heroes. So, it may also be used for deceased people; and also for initiated human souls. The point here is missed by many translators. It is not saying, as in Rieu's version, "as immortals **come in** by this way", because no direction of motion is specified by Homer at all. No reference is made to descending at all. Homer simply states that, "Rather it is the path for immortals." And, since it is reserved for spiritual beings, the possibility arises that this interface is one where beings **ascend out of matter**.

So let's see the passage again, correctly translated,

> Moreover at the head of this harbour is an olive tree, capable of fruit-bearing; and near to this, {is} a cave – misty and delightful, sacred to the nymphs known as the Naiades.
> And in this (cave) are mixing bowls and amphorae, of stone.
> And there, moreover, wild bees store honey.
> In it (the cave) are tall marble looms, for there nymphs weave cloth, of crimson – a wonder to behold.
> And water flows unceasingly in this cave.
> And two openings it has. By the one to the north, humans descend.
> The one to the south is divine, men do not enter by that place, at all. Rather it is (an opening for) the path used by immortals.

So this section of the great epic is a veiled account of the process of incarnating. To learn the nature of how the soul merges into flesh is an important part of spiritual wisdom, revealing much of value to the acolyte. In particular, there is a specific need to experience the way our consciousness changes as we leave the spiritual realms, to enter down into earthly consciousness. This experience teaches one how the cognitional processes change to adapt to the nature of the sense organs and the brain. Gaining spiritual perception is in effect, a reversal of that process.

About 1,050 years later, the great neo-Platonist, Porphyry (232-305 AD), wrote a commentary on this Cave of the Nymphs, and to help explain his interpretation, he included the text of an ancient hymn from the Mysteries of Apollo. It is wonderful that he did this, because no other copy survived, it was otherwise lost to posterity.

APPENDIX

The beginning of HOMER'S ODYSSEY
An exact, literal translation by Adrian Anderson Ph.D.,
establishing the accuracy of Rudolf Steiner's interpretation.

Ἄνδρα μοι ἔννεπε, μοῦσα, πολύτροπον, ὃς μάλα πολλὰ
Andra moi ennepe mousa polotropon hos mala polla
Of the man, tell me, Muse, {he} much travelled, who very much

πλάγχθη, ἐπεὶ Τροίης ἱερὸν πτολίεθρον ἔπερσεν·
wandered-astray, since he attacked the sacred citadel of Troy.

πολλῶν δ' ἀνθώπων ἴδεν ἄστεα καὶ νόον ἔγνω,
poloen d' anthroepoen iden astea kai no-on egnoe
Many of people cities he saw, and customs he learnt.

Πολλὰ δ' ὅ γ' ἐν πόντῳ
polla d ho g en pontoe
many And {it} also, at sea/in the sea,

πάθεν ἄλγεα
pathen algea
mental torments he suffered in his feelings,

ὃν κατὰ θυμόν,
hon kata thumon
this throughout his passions,

ἀρνύμενος ἥν τε ψυχὴν καὶ νόσον ἑταίρων.
arnumenos haen te psuchaen kai noson hetairoen
to gain with honour *that* soul, and the home-coming of
comrades.

ἀλλ' οὐδ' ὣς ἑτάρους ἐρρύσατο, ἱέμενός περ.
all' oud hoes hetarous errusato hiemenos per
But none of the comrades did he rescue, however much he tried.

CHAPTER FOUR   Porphyry; A lost Hymn to Apollo, its initiatory message

In his commentary on the Cave of the Nymphs mentioned by Homer in the Odyssey (Book 13), Porphyry provides his readers with the text of this otherwise lost hymn. He mentions this hymn as part of his argument to show that the role of the nymphs (or water sprites) in creation is central to the Homeric passage. The hymn to Apollo is very valuable in clarifying the mystical worldview of the ancient Mysteries. But to see its real value, the message in this ambiguous text has to be discerned.

Here we present a new translation, which we believe reveals the initiatory meaning of this hymn for the first time. There are very few books with a translation of this text. The florid English translation by Taylor from the 18th century of this passage is widely used in alternative spiritual circles, but its value is reduced because its English is by now quite dated. The version made by Lamberton and colleagues, and the French translation by P. Saintyves, are not focussed on the esoteric meaning. But difficulties in working with this text are not surprising, as it is very complex grammatically, and as a highly esoteric text, inherently difficult to understand.

The hymn actually concerns a primary theme from the Mysteries, and also from later Gnosticism. That is, the inherent conflict between spiritual realities and earthly matter, especially the earth-bound consciousness it produces in people once they descend into birth. Despite Porphyry's convictions to the contrary, this wonderful hymn has little to do with water-spirits (nymphs), but a lot to do with proclaiming the existence of ethereal streams of spiritual energies which permeate matter, and which help to uplift human consciousness to spiritual realities, even though people are encased in a material body.

In Greek myths, Apollo is a central god with regard to attaining to spirituality, or one could say, to the higher self. He seeks to help people to attain this, and the Muses are his assistants. He can be regarded as a symbol of the sun god – the great central deity of antiquity.

The hymn reads in my translation,

The Hymn to Apollo:

And so for Thee, springs of flowing
spiritual-intelligence well forth,
located within caves, nurturing the Earth
by the divine inspiration of the Muse's
oracular utterance –
itself proceeding from a divine voice.
And these spiritual-energies break through
beyond the earth's surface,
by flowing everywhere,
thus conferring on mortals
the perpetual outpourings of sweet streams. [27]

Rudolf Steiner's commentary on Apollo is invaluable here, to understand what this remarkable text is conveying. Steiner taught that Apollo's spiritual task for humanity was to work with the spiritual sunlight and guide it to the Earth. The Muses are spiritual beings who help Apollo, and are grouped around him. Steiner taught that Apollo is very important spiritual being who in ancient epochs, harmonized the threefold mind of human beings.

The hymn is making the remarkable assertion that, for the sake of Apollo – which means for the sake of what Apollo would like humanity to spiritually achieve – there actually exists on the Earth ethereal streams or currents which are animated with a spiritual intelligence. This is in deep harmony with the above statement from Steiner that Apollo was active as a mediator to the Earth of the spiritual forces from the spiritual sun. In this Apollonian hymn, the word 'caves' appears to mean actual caves, or the subterranean realms, that is the Earth's mineral crust, which is seen as permeated by currents of certain subtle energies.

These subtle streams of ethereal energies are said to nurture matter from out of the ether. This is different to the metaphorical 'cave' at Ithaca in the Odyssey, where nymphs are mentioned, and where they are described as weaving flesh around the embryonic skeleton. There no real cave is meant. But here the mineral crust of the Earth is meant.

In this hymn to Apollo, no nymphs are mentioned. The Taylor translation has simply added the phrase, 'the Nymphs residing

_____

[27] Greek text available at: http://www.scribd.com/doc/5563193

in caves shall...' because that was Taylor's conviction. Now, the above phrase, 'flowing spiritual-intelligence' in Greek is literally, 'intellectual waters'; which is of course a physical impossibility. So the expression is a metaphor. This phrase presents a striking image of streams of spiritual energies, imbued with consciousness or intelligence, flowing behind matter, flowing on an energy level, existing behind molecular substance.

The term 'spiritual intelligence' is unusual, but it is similar to terms used in mystical circles today about spirit beings and energies in spirit realms. People in these groups use such expressions as 'living thoughts' or 'thought-forms' or 'currents of golden light' that are imbued with consciousness. The term, 'intellectual' here, referring to fountains of "intellectual waters" {νοερῶν ὑδάτων}, means the capacity of being conscious, of possessing a soul or mind. Both humans as well as spiritual beings were thought of as possessing a soul. Hence spiritual beings of the planetary spheres were called 'intelligences'.

This phrase, "intellectual waters" is similar to a term used by another esotericist, Zosimus Panopolitanos, an alchemist, namely, 'divine water' {ὕδατος θείου}. This mystic was writing at approximately the same time as Porphyry. The term occurs, misplaced, on a page in his treatise about alchemy and the sensory-organs. [28] The term, 'water' in both these texts means 'subtle energies', since water flows so freely and discreetly, thereby resembling ethereal currents.

In this hymn, these 'streams' are said to be located in caves, but this means the dense matter of the earthly realm. The caves represent the material realm, and the streams themselves are metaphors for spiritual energies. This refers to precisely those spiritual energies which derive from the sun and which Apollo guided to the Earth.

In so far as these streams of spiritual energies can permeate people, they are thereby assisting or nurturing the Earth, which is the home of people who have come down into incarnation from the celestial realms. So the inspiring and reverential message from the Apollo priesthood is this: matter is not the only factor here on Earth, in which we 'live and move have our being', for there are helpful spiritual energies here, too. And it is

---

[28] This Greek text of Zosimus Panopoltanos in Hermetica, edit./tran. W. Scott , vol 4, p. 104   Shambhala, Boston 1985.

due to the influence of Apollo that these energies are present in the earthly sphere.

But we also learn from this initiatory hymn that these currents of spiritual-intelligence are resonating to the tones or speech which come from the Muses. In Greek myths, the Muses are the companions of Apollo; in the lovely language of Greek myth, 'they sing to his lyre'. We are told that the tones emanating from the Muses are in turn themselves inspired from a divine source, from high spiritual wisdom. This divine voice no doubt refers to the 'music of the spheres', which could be thought of as 'the divine Fiat'. It is the cosmic wisdom that pervades creation.

So now we begin to see what the lofty wisdom of the Apollo priesthood is really communicating here. These currents of spiritual energies, inwardly resonating to distant celestial tones, surge along, passing through mineral substances and move on, to permeate human beings. And in doing this, they are giving to sensitive people an awareness of spiritual realities, or at least of higher ideas. In the symbolic language of the hymn, they surge upwards, beyond the surface of the Earth, out of the 'caves', and then into people. Their influence is described as delightful or sweet, indicating their uplifting and spiritualizing nature.

So, the hymn, when understood in this way, provides a remarkable glimpse into the Mystery wisdom of the Grecian Mysteries dedicated to Apollo. See the Appendix for a more detailed analysis of the grammar here, and the differences in the various translations.

Finally, before we leave the Grecian era behind, we will just briefly note another great sage of this era, Iamblichus. In the 4th century AD he also established a spiritual centre, possibly located in Syria. He established a standard curriculum for such studies as his, and he imposed a systematic method of interpreting Plato. He extended the use of mathematical ideas in philosophy. He also refined the esoteric doctrines derived from the Neo-Platonists (the later followers of Plato), and incorporated into his Neoplatonic philosophy selected ideas from the spiritual worldview of earlier mystical systems.

The end of the Mysteries
The new dynamic which arose in the Greco-Latin Age, of individualized intellectual activity, creating a contrast between the mystics and the philosophers, was to get ever stronger as

the centuries passed by. Although the various Mysteries of the Grecian Age were deeply respected, and drew large crowds at their public festivals, as historians of the Hellenistic times make clear, only a small percentage of the populace actually underwent initiation into the spiritual realities that the Mysteries offered. There was now, in great contrast to previous Ages, a dualism arising in society. A more intellectual age was dawning, and the Mysteries were starting to fade.

There were those who still retained interest in the sacred, the transcendent, but there were many who were no longer seriously interested in the spiritual side of life. No longer would the populace agree to work as one unified group under the control of the priesthoods, to construct great initiatory sites with intricate cosmic alignments, and extraordinary engineering challenges, around which the most privileged people would have burial sites. In looking at history in this different way, that is, as the means for the evolving of human consciousness, a new perspective on the meaning of human life arises. It gives a clue as to why from the time of ancient Greece onwards, great sacred sites became a thing of the past.

One can now conclude that long ago, in the age of the Egyptian Old Kingdom, of the European Celts at their Externsteine site, and with the Megalithic sites of Britain, it was the case that in general, people revered the most, and were the most influenced by, their high priests.
These were the people whom they regarded as the most clairvoyant – **and hence the most cosmically attuned**.
But now in the Greek era, people began to respect as the greatest minds, those who were most brilliantly logical – **and hence the least psychically aware, the least holistically inclined**.

In fact, as we shall see, as the Grecian influence began to wane, around 400 AD, the Mysteries were outlawed in Christendom. This new paradigm of personal intellectual ability started in ancient Greece and became the norm in the West from the Italian Renaissance, and especially from the Industrial Revolution onwards, when scientists were given a high social status.

A return to the older pattern started in the 1960's, with a revival of interest in spirituality. In today's world, we have a mixture of the above. For many people the most sharp, brilliant logical-scientific mind is the most admirable, to others the more holistic attitude, seeking spirituality is the more admirable. What this implies for the modern world and its spiritual problems will be considered another time. Firstly, we need to understand more about the origin of today's materialistic mindset.

The legend of Cyprian and Justina

We will now consider a valuable and fascinating text, of great significance in understanding why esoteric spirituality to a great extent died out towards the end of the Greco-Latin Age. This text is a pious Christian legend, a work of fiction, called The Legend of Cyprian and Justina. The legend existed in various versions dating from about AD 250 to AD 350, and texts survive in three separate documents. It is designed to persuade people of the superiority of Christianity over the old esoteric wisdom and practices.

But in reporting on the esoteric beliefs of the man Cyprian, these texts actually preserve for posterity rare glimpses into the highly esoteric knowledge and experiences of people initiated in the Mysteries. (The legend also preserves superstitious beliefs and practices of the time.) In about AD 450 a Byzantine empress, called Eudocia, wrote a very long poem based on these documents. This story is entirely fictional, but it is based on real knowledge as to the experiences occurring to those who were initiated in the Mysteries.

The legend tells of the esoteric interests and occult abilities of a young man who falls in love with a Christian woman, and how he tries to use these powers to win her love. But her Christianity protects her and eventually converts Cyprian, who then joins the church. We shall consider a few brief extracts, from the poem by Empress Eudocia, which tell of Cyprian's 'confession' as he converts to Christianity through the influence of Justina:

> And 20 yrs of age was I when I journeyed to Egypt... I went to Memphis, where I learned of things by nature far beyond the earthly. I learnt of the {ethereal} terrestrial forces, how they combine with each other; of the remote {i.e., planetary} spirits – their intelligence and names, and with what planet they are associated. I learnt the laws that govern these spirits, and what are their tasks. How they flee from darkness and yet dwell in darknesses.
> I was man of 30 years now as I left the land of Egypt and guided my path to the ancient city of the Chaldeans.

Here I wanted to learn how the heavens revolve, and also the pathways of the stars. There I learnt about the stars; their associations one with another, the astrological houses to which they belong.

And I learnt too how, impelled by love, lofty spirit beings gather and create within rays of light....sages taught me of these things.... I came to {the mystery centre at} Elis,[29] and I came to Sparta and saw the clumsy idol, made of wood, of Artemis Tauropolos. And thus I learnt diverse properties of matter, the nature of metals, and of {gem}stones.... [30]

We see here how this text is presented by the ruling church authority as a self-evident presentation of how the Mysteries provided reprehensible skills or superstitious knowledge, involving demonic beings. But actually, the text presents a fine outline of the kind of wholesome spiritual insights which the Mysteries bestowed. We see that in the Mysteries a subtle elemental energy was believed to exist behind matter. This was explored, as well as the qualities these energies bestow on gemstones.

It is interesting to compare this extract from the poem, with the same episode about Memphis, translated from the older original versions,

"After these things, when I was twenty years old, I came to Egypt, to Memphis, and there in the initiatory sanctuaries, I took up an {initiatory} ordeal about the spirit beings who are located in the spheres surrounding the Earth. {I learnt} about in what place {in the celestial spheres} they ward off evil.   (translated the author)

Although with this legend, the church is wanting to condemn the Mystery wisdom, these revelations are about a high level of spiritual experience. Before this Egyptian episode, the texts tell us that Cyprian was in Athens, and the older texts report that Cyprian recalls that this is "where I was initiated concerning the Seven Hierophants, namely as to their cosmic spiritual

---

[29] At a place called Elis a student of Socrates had founded a small mystery school.
[30] From a German translation of the poem by Eudocia by F. Gregorovius, in Athenais, F. A. Brockhaus, Leipzig, 1882.

energies...".[31] This appears to refer to becoming acquainted with planetary influences, as understood in classical astrology.

The next extract comes from the long poem written by Eudocia, and presents some linguistic problems to the translator, because the Greek is very obscure, but it is of real value to those interested in the initiatory experiences of the Hellenistic world. It is published in the official writings of the church fathers (the Migne collection). It reads in my translation like this:

> I learnt of amulets and of {esoteric} images
> – and the script of the cosmos –
> and of earthly myths...[32]

Here in these words one discovers that such an acolyte also learnt to decipher the secret language of imagery, that is, esoteric symbols and graphics. Graphic images were often used in the Mysteries, because in this way the knowledge could be kept secret, for even though others may see it, they could not understand the imagery. Such graphics were also used to assist the acolyte to develop a higher more visual, less analytical consciousness. This more pictorial mindset is important as the experiences awaiting the acolyte involved psychically seeing various bewildering images of spiritual realities.

The statement that Cyprian learnt "the script of the cosmos" or the 'cosmic script' is especially intriguing. The phrase here in Greek is literally, 'the characters of the cosmos'; meaning 'characters' in the sense of letters.[33] Rudolf Steiner often used the expression, 'to read the cosmic script', and much of anthroposophy is in effect the result of this spiritual discerning or 'reading'. This is an expression which obviously refers to the motions and relations of planets and stars to each other, and their influences upon the realms of nature. To learn "to read the script of the cosmos" was no doubt a specific part of spiritual development in many esoteric systems. The illustration shows the first page of the Greek poem in which all this occurs, created by Eudocia about AD 450.

---

[31] The Greek text has word for energies here (ἐνέργειαν) which is used in ancient Grecian spiritual texts for the energy or influence of spiritual beings) and this is often specifically of a cosmic kind.
[32] Greek text of the official 'Confession of Cyprian" in Migne: Patrologia vol. CCX (V) METANOIA TOU AGIOU KUPRIANOU pages 296 – 329.
[33] In Eudocia's Greek: χαρακτῆρας δέ τε κόσμου

From Tibetan mandalas and Australian Aboriginal designs, to the Icelandic Runes, and the patterns created by Megalithic standing stones, graphics were an integral part of conveying and veiling the mystical knowledge of that culture. The Tarot cards are also an example of this technique, deriving from ancient Egyptian days.

Finally, we note that our 'miscreant acolyte' also learnt to understand earthly myths. This is an interesting statement, as it means that he was taught the key to understanding mythological stories. The stories in the mythology of a nation derive from the Mysteries and are described by Hellenistic writers as actually veiled ways of communicating the Mystery wisdom. One has to be taught the key in order to discover their inner meaning.

Myths are a way to present initiatory truths to the public in a gentler form, which may arouse interest in some listeners as to what the deeper narrative is. The mythic story of Jonah or of Perseus descending into the Underworld is a way of communicating that an initiatory experience takes one into the lower self, which, in contrast to the somewhat abstract Jungian views, is not a metaphor, but a real experience of an objective spirit realm, where various beings who resonate with one's own lower qualities objectively exist.

Now, the legend goes on to tell how Cyprian tried to force the Christian lady Justina to fall in love with him, by using his magical powers, but he fails because, as the legend triumphantly points out, the power of Christ in Justina's soul is superior to that of the 'pagan' gods of the Mysteries in Cyprian's soul. Consequently, and this is the main message of this legend, the pagan initiate Cyprian then converts to Christianity. The basis of this legend is very probably some form of hostility between the Christian church and the Mysteries which was occurring already by AD 250. [34]

From these documents we can learn various significant facts about what the ancient Mysteries actually bestowed upon its acolytes, in the way of access to the spirit realms. But one also sees another fact - that about AD 250 antagonism was already felt by the Church authorities towards the Mysteries, and thus

---

[34] R. Reitzenstein, Cyprian der Magier 11. Nov 1916, Göttingen Nachrichten, 1917, and Ryan Baily, The *Confessio* of Cyprian of Antioch, McGill University, Masters Thesis, 2009

also towards the rites and processions held at their various sacred sites. Very significantly, by 450 AD this antagonism becomes a potent reality, for by now the Church had become the State.

At this point we need to understand a new development in the spiritual life of the Greco-Latin Age, which we have not deal with before – the forming of the new religion, Christianity. This event was to have a hugely negative impact on, and yet contains a hidden link to, the sacred places of the Mysteries across the Hellenistic world. As we can see from the above extract of the legend about Cyprian, this new religion lived in an antagonistic tension with the Mystery religions.

The rise of Christianity
The mystical worldview of the priesthoods who worked in the Mysteries, and their effect upon the cultural life of the Greco-Latin is a large subject. But so too are the central themes and spiritual values (or theological convictions) of Christendom. Many profound and sacred themes are involved in the study of Christianity – especially for those who respond to the profound ethical and mystical truths in it.

For people with an esoteric awareness, a deeper message of a profoundly spiritual nature can be found in the core texts of this new religion, when contemplated in their original Greek. If the Christian texts are approached with knowledge of other ancient spiritual texts from this period, such as the Nag Hammadi or Hermetic-Gnostic texts, then a deeper, more mystical view on Christianity arises, which has some points of contact with the ancient Mysteries – in their best phase.

Most of the theological work done in Christianity is based on a very limited feeling for this deeper mystical-esoteric side. However, this is not to undervalue the work done by Christian scholars, both from many centuries ago, and those who as from the 1850's began to develop textual analysis of the scriptures in a rigorously objective process. This is known as the 'text-critical method', and it developed from such incisive minds as Theodor Zahn, F. Godet and Heinrich A.W. Meyer, whose 19 volume New Testament commentary is still immensely valuable today.

ΜΕΤΑΝΟΙΑ
ΤΟΥ ΑΓΙΟΥ ΚΥΠΡΙΑΝΟΥ.

ΟΣΟΙ τοῖς τῷ Χριστῷ μυςηρίοις [a] προσκό-
πτετε, τοῖς ἐμοῖς δάκρυσιν ἐπιβλέψατε, κỳ
γνῶτε πάντων τῶν ἐμφερομένων ἐν αὐτοῖς τὴν
δύναμιν. ὅσοι τοῖς δαιμονικοῖς ἐπιτέρπεσθε τρό-
ποις, παρ᾽ ἐμοῦ μάθετε τὴν ματαιότητα τῶν ἐν
αὐτοῖς [b] χλευασμάτων. οὔτε γὰρ ὑμῶν ἐμοῦ
δεισιδαιμονέστερός ποτε γνωσθῆναι δυνήσεται, οὔτε
διερευνήσασθαι τὰ περὶ θεῶν τῶν λεγομένων,
οὔτε ἐφικέσθαι τῆς παρ᾽ αὐτῶν ἐνεργείας. ἐγώ εἰ-
μι Κυπριανὸς, ὁ ἐξ ἀπαλῶν ὀνύχων ἀνατεθεὶς
τῷ Ἀπόλλωνι κειμήλιον, μηθεὶς ἔτι τύπος τῆ
τῷ δράκοντος δραματουργίαν. ἔτι οὔπω ἥμην
ἐτῶν ὅτι [c] τοῖς τῆ Μίθρου προσῆλθον μυστη-
ρείοις, κỳ ὡς [d] Ἀθηναῖος ἐπήλυτος ὤν, ὑπὸ δὲ
τῶν γεννησάντων με διὰ σπουδῆς πολίτης γνώ-
μῳνος, ἔτι ὢν δέκα ἐτῶν, ἐδαδούχησα τῆ Δη-
μήτρα, κỳ [e] τῆς κόρης τὸ λευκὸν πένθος ὑπέμει-
να, κỳ τῆς ἐν τῆ ἀκροπόλει Παλλάδος [f] τῷ
δράκοντι ἐλειτούργησα, εἰς προσκοπὴν [g] νεωκό-
ρου καταςάς. ἐξῳχόμην κỳ ἐν τῷ Ὀλυμπίῳ ὄρει,
τῶν θεῶν, ὡς λέγουσι, [h] οἰκητήριον, κỳ ἐμυή-
θην ἤχοις ὁμιλιῶν κỳ ψόφων δήμων· εἶδον ἐκεῖ
φαντάζοντα πρέμνα, κỳ πόας ἐνεργεῖν δοκούσας
θεὰν ὑπισκοπαῖς. εἶδον ἐκεῖ ὡρῶν διαδοχὰς, πνευ-
μάτων ὑπαλλασσόντων, κỳ ἡμερῶν διαφορότητα
ὑπό τινων ἐνεργείων ἐναντίων [i] συνισταμένων. εἶδον ἐκεῖ χορεῖς δαιμόνων ὑμνούντων, κỳ ἄλλων
πολεμούντων, κỳ ἑτέρων [k] ἐνεδρευόντων, ἀπα-
τώντων, συγχεόντων, κỳ ἑκάςου θεοῦ κỳ θεᾶς
ἐθεασάμην ἐκεῖ τὴν φάλαγγα, μείνας αὐτόθι
ἡμέρας τεσσαράκοντα· ὁπόθεν ὡς ἐκ βασιλείων
ἀποςέλλονται τὰ πράγματα, ἐνεργεῖν ἕκαςον αὐτῶν ἐν τῆ γῆ κỳ ἐν πᾶσι τοῖς ἔθνεσι· ἐσιτιζό-
μην [l] ἀκρόδρυα μόνον μετὰ δύσιν ἡλίου. κỳ δὴ

---

[f] Τῷ δράκοντι] Non belle Oxoniensis editor dæmonem
hoc in loco, ut in pluribus aliis ejusdem libri, generatim
draconis nomine designari existimat. Liquet hic indicari
draconem illum, qui Athenis in templo Minervæ colebatur.
Narrat Plutarchus in Themistoclis vita pag. 282. Themi-
stoclem, cum Atheniensibus persuadere vellet, ut relicta
urbe in naves secederent, inito cum sacerdotibus consilio
persecisse, ut dracone his diebus in adytis non apparente,
& libaminibus, quæ ei quotidie apponebantur, integris re-
pertis, Minerva dereliquisse urbem, & ducem se civibus ad
mare præbere videretur.

[g] Νεωκόρου] Vetus interpres hæc conjungit cum iis quæ
sequuntur: Et post promotionem sacerdos constitutus sum in
Olympio monte. Hæc autem promotio non ætatis, ut editori
Oxon. videtur, sed dignitatis accessionem designat.

[h] Οἰκητήριον] Lege οἰκητήρειω.

[i] Συνισταμένων] Legendum videtur συνισταμένω. Dierum
autem varietatem nequaquam hic scriptor dæmonibus at-
tribuit, sed ait eos sibi illam attribuisse in visionibus quas ei
objiciebant.

[k] Ἐνεδρευόντων] Obsessa facientium, Oxon. obscena facientium, Thes.

[l] Ἀκρόδρυα] Sic redditur in edit. Oxon. summa tenera de
arboribus. Summa tenera de roboribus Thes.

The original Greek of the
Legend of Cyprian &
Justina, from Empress
Eudocia, AD 450.

A rare & valuable fragment
about the Mysteries,
preserved in a text
designed to condemn the
esoteric heritage of
the Hellenistic Age.

48

It has continued on into the present time and flourishes through Karl Rahner, Eduard Schweizer and Ulrich Lux, to mention a few. Our exploration of the new religion's impact on the Mysteries will be undertaken with an awareness of the fact which we have noted in this book, that changes occur in human consciousness over the ages. This process changed the way that people related to the spiritual, just at the time that this new religion was being formed.

We will discover that there is, although unknown to the Christian world generally, a deeply mystical or initiatory aspect hidden in the Greek texts of the new religion. This hidden aspect teaches that the events that happened on Golgotha hill, the Crucifixion and Resurrection, have similarities with the core process in the Mysteries of antiquity; but on a cosmic scale. We shall gradually discover what these similarities are.

An initiatory process was undertaken in the pyramids of Egypt, and at the Externsteine, and in old Celtic sites in Alsace, in Bulgaria, and elsewhere. Details about this process are not available, as all such matters were kept confidential. But from the sparse references to the Mysteries, which we noted earlier it is clear that the acolyte was put through a form of training involving many trials, to prepare themselves for a direct encounter with the spiritual realms.

Rudolf Steiner taught that the core initiatory experience of the Mysteries involved the acolyte undergoing an out-of-the-body spiritual journey, whilst the body lay in a sarcophagus. Steiner emphasizes that this process actually occupied three days. During the three days, the acolyte lay as if dead, whilst their soul descended into the Underworld, and then ascended into divine realms. At the end of the three days, they would awaken as an enlightened person, who had experienced a kind of resurrection of themselves, bestowing on them a higher state of consciousness. So they underwent a kind of death and resurrection. At each of the sacred sites mentioned above, the Externsteine, the Rhodope Mountains area of Bulgaria, and the Great Pyramid, (and probably at other sites not yet discovered or researched) there was a very prominent ceremonial sarcophagus, which had no lid. These were no doubt used for this mystical purpose, and not for burials.

In the next chapter, we shall consider some of the evidence for a three-day process wherein the acolyte in a symbolic sense died and then was resurrected as an initiate. Here we can note that this time-span of three days is not only indicated in some rare mystical documents, but also in a document written by a Hellenistic herbal doctor.

A letter written by one Thessalus, a herbal doctor from the 1st century AD has survived, wherein the doctor recommends himself to the Emperor Claudius. But the letter suggests that Asklepios, the god of healing himself, helped to write it. Thessalus tells the Emperor that he travelled to the Egyptian town of Thebes, in order to seek initiation from the priests there into the spiritual secrets of healing and medicine, and this would involve encountering Asklepios.

Thessalus reports that he underwent an initiatory time (referred to as fasting), which lasted for three-days. After this time, he was able to clairvoyantly behold the god of healing. The deity then revealed to him the secrets of plants and their links to the spiritual forces in the cosmos. So the letter's reference to Thessalus being placed in a special condition for three days, affirms a three-day core initiatory process, although a mystical sleep as such is not referred to.[35]

The mystical religions of Egypt and of Greece provided some insight into their secret knowledge, through publicly available myths. These myths usually told of a battle between good and evil powers, and which resulted in the good deity, (Osiris, Attis, Adonis, etc) dying for three-days, and then coming back to life. After a three-day sleep comes a resurrection, bringing new life and blessings to the people of that community.

From other comments about the Mysteries it is clear that this archetypal process was also undergone by an acolyte, often called a 'hero' in the myths who encountered the god, but only after first encountering their lower self. So there is the implication that the community had access, through the priests, to a deity who undertakes through some form of sacrifice to bring spiritual renewal to the people, giving the community a more wholesome life situation.

Moreover, by having a good link to the deity, the people could expect to have protection from evil powers after death. But those who sought to attain a high spirituality by undergoing the

---

[35] The letter is given in "Judaism and Hellenism, Studies in their Encounter in Palestine during the early Hellenistic period", by M. Hengel; the ancient Greek text is in Catalogus Codicum Astrologorum Graecorum, 8:3, 1912, ps 134ff.

three-day sleep process could seek to have communion with the deity **before their lifetime ended**. And if such a communion became possible, then the acolyte could expect a much more enhanced, a more wonderful existence after death. To achieve this, the acolyte had to go through the initiatory process.

A fine confirmation of what the Mysteries, at their best, sought to offer their members in this regard, is left for posterity in an engraving found at Eleusis, by a certain Glaucus, who was a hierophant at Eleusis until advanced old age,

> Beautiful indeed is the Mystery given to us by the blessed gods; death is for {initiated} mortals no longer an evil, but a blessing. [36]

---

[36] The Mystery religions, S. Angus, Dover, N.Y. 1975, p.140.

Appendix

More about the Hymn to Apollo

It is possible to render this verse, as does Prof. Lamberton, so that it is the nymphs in caves in the earth who are nursed to divine utterance by the inspiration of the Muse, but this does not appear to be the intended meaning. We should note here that Taylor has literally added the phrase, "The Nymphs residing in..." and Lamberton has taken up this addition. But the ancient hymn, as given by Porphyry, does not contain these words at all.

Nymphs are not directly mentioned in the original, and it is unlikely, given their minor status, that they would be involved in giving utterance of divine truths emanating from the cosmos, or giving 'sweet currents' of spiritual energies to people everywhere up above, on the surface of the planet, far from their springs. But above all, since the 'springs' are not springs of physical water, nymphs are not involved, so this interpretation is flawed.

It is also possible to render this verse, as does the French scholar, P. Saintyves, so that the spiritual waters flowing in the caves, and indeed giving 'sweet currents' of spiritual energies, are nourished by the breath of the Earth, on behalf of the oracles. But this suggests that earthly matter itself (i.e., subterranean caverns) contains the breath of the Earth, and that this could somehow be nourishing for others; this is also very unlikely. This interpretation also appears not to be the intended meaning.

And finally, Taylor's version is not so helpful here; his 18th century use of English is too antiquated and his style too florid to convey a clear meaning to this text. His treatment of the Homeric passage from the Odyssey is especially unhelpful. The other translations are as follows,

Thom. Taylor (1730),

> The Nymphs residing in caves shall deduce fountains of intellectual waters (according to the divine voice of the Muses), which are the progeny of a terrene spirit. Hence waters, bursting through every river, shall exhibit to mankind perpetual effusions of sweet streams.
> (Reprinted Phanes Press 1991)

French version by Professor P. Saintyves,

> For Thee, fountains of spiritual waters constantly flow in
> the caves, nourished by the breath of the Earth, on behalf of
> the oracles, the divineness of the Muse. And on the ground,
> {the fountains} flowing in all directions confers on mortals
> of their sweet water, the continual effusions.   (Published
> Emile, Nourry, Editeur, 62 Rue des Ecoles, 1918)
> (Translated by A. Anderson)

Professor R. Lamberton   Univ. Chicago,

> They who live in caves in the earth, nursed to divine
> utterance by the inspiration of the Muse, have made springs
> of water of wisdom flow for you, and break through the
> earth in all the glens, bringing to men the unceasing flow of
> their sweet streams.   (Published Station Hill Press, 1983

Technically the question of who is being nurtured (or nursed/nourished) is pivotal to understanding this passage. Lamberton sees this as the nymphs, but as we have noted above, there are no nymphs in the hymn; they were assumed by Porphyry. To Saintyves, it is the spiritual waters which the breath of the earth is nourishing. But in both of these cases, the nurturing activity is present in an active way. But the verb underlying the term here, (ἀτῖταλλω) is a 'passive voice' verb in terms of Attic (and also Hellenistic) Greek grammar, and with these verbs, the default condition of the subject of the verb is genitive. In my translation the nurturing is in the passive sense, and the noun, the earth (γαίης) in the genitive; in the other versions, the nouns are dative.

CHAPTER FIVE: The descent into the Underworld

Three-day initiatory sleep in Greece

We noted that the Mysteries offered a three-day sleep process, which was a replication of the three-day 'death' of the god of that sacred site. We saw how in this era, people were deeply anxious about the after-life, about what happens after death – as Agamemnon made clear with his remarks about preferring to be a poverty-stricken person here, than a king in the Underworld. It becomes clear now that the Mysteries in the Greco-Latin epoch are highly valued for the effect that they will have upon empowering the person with regard to the after-life, as well as for the experience of divinities and the attainment of wisdom.

There is a notable saying about the symbiotic link of the death process and the initiation process, which probably derives from Plutarch a priest at the shrine of Delphi, who was also a famous historian. His words are preserved in the writings of an anthologist, Johannes of Stobae (5th century AD), "The soul at death undergoes an experience similar to those who undergo great initiations...".[37] Now, it is also the case that in ancient cultures, and in some ethnic cultures of today, the death process is said to occupy three-days, similar to the initiatory sleep. Often in such cultures, a three-day funeral process is observed.

In the ancient Mysteries, as Rudolf Steiner explains, the soul or rather the body, was put into in a kind of sleep state for three-days, whilst the soul, freed of the body, underwent a soul journey,

> All the various peoples of antiquity had Mysteries...the acolyte was prepared through soul-exercises for a long time so that they could go through this process of being 'laid in the grave'. The hierophant was able to bring the acolyte into higher states of consciousness, as his body lay (in the sarcophagus or on a cross) in a deep sleep for three days. The soul was then guided through the regions of the spiritual realm and after three days brought back. He felt himself to be a new (re-born)

---

[37] Plutarch, Fragments 178, from Johannes of Stobae, Anthology 4.52.49, in M. Meyer, Ancient Mysteries.

person. He received a new name. He was thereafter called a 'son of god'.[38]

The after-life and the initiatory process are closely linked, as the person whose body has died also undertakes a journey through the spiritual realms. Hence the sacred sites used for the after-life and for initiation were often close to each other. That the actual death process results in a three-day process where the soul is separating from the body at the end of which the soul is ready for its journey, is widely indicated in the customs and writings of many cultures. So the initiatory process in extending over three days was replicating this, working in with a mysterious dynamic inherent in human nature.

This theme of a descent into the underworld within the Grecian Mysteries is not based on any assumption, it was a formal part of Greek religious life. Known as the 'katabasis', which means the descent into the Netherworld, it was a feature of many sacred sites. However, in the myths, initiation is described in a simplified way, so the three-day sleep and other secrets of the initiatory process are not referred to in detail. At the oracle of Trophonius, situated at Lebadea, it was widely known that such descents into the Netherworld were the means by which the priests provided the wisdom that was being sought. Quite a number of semi-mythical early heroes undertook the three-day initiatory process, and these experiences are likewise described in the myths, in a simplified way. Such heroes include Musaios and Eumolpos, and the famous Hercules, who were initiated at Eleusis, and reports circulated to the effect that the great sage Pythagoras went through this process, too.

The three-day initiatory sleep in the Hebrew world
We have seen that the initiatory sleep process involving three days is affirmed by the three-day pattern in the stories of the gods of the various Mysteries. There is the famous story in the Bible, of the Hebrew mystic or prophet Jonah, who was swallowed by a whale, and then three days later was spat out onto the seashore. This story is seen by people in the western mystical tradition as a disguised way of telling 'those in the know' about this very process.

In this view, the sea then symbolizes the spirit world. Now this esoteric interpretation of the legend of Jonah is not without foundation; there is really substantial evidence in the Biblical

---

[38] From a lecture given 2nd Dec. 1906 in Cologne.

story itself. For in the words that Jonah speaks whilst in his experience, in his prayer to God for help, there are some puzzling references, carefully intermingled with more normal imagery:

> ...From the depths of Sheol, I called for help, and you listened to my cry. You hurled me into the deep, into the very heart of the seas, and the currents swirled about me; all your waves and breakers swept over me...in the troughs of mountains I was sinking into a realm whose bars would hold me forever. But you brought my life up from the pit, O Lord my God.   (Book of Jonah 2:2-6)

In this text Jonah identifies his location as the Sheol, but 'Sheol' is the Hebrew name for the realm of the Dead, also known as the Underworld ! It is not the term for the stomach of a whale, nor for the marine world. This is very significant. And Jonah also refers to being amidst the roots or troughs of mountains – this is not where whales normally descend. Illustration One is a 14th century naïve painting of this story. Inside its belly, Jonah could not know about the outside environment. This text gives the impression of Jonah being in the foundations or substratum of the earth, but on a spiritual level.

It is very likely that this is what is meant, because in similar literature from the old Hebrews and Greeks, the lower, after-life realms were described as located deep inside the Earth. And moreover, the really evil realms were located below these, forming the deepest foundations of the Earth. We find this idea also in the Book of Job (26:5). In this text there is a reference to the dead in their dreary Sheol,

> ...the dead in deep anguish – those beneath the waters (the wicked), and {those} that live in the waters (the normal deceased souls).

The earlier mystics would feel that if a person were to experience such dreadful realms, whilst out of their body, then they would feel as if in "a realm whose bars would hold me forever." In fact, it was a common belief in the Hellenistic world, that the very interior of the Earth was a kind of barred prison where evil beings were kept; they had been cast down there by the good gods.

1   Jonah released from the whale after 3 days
An illustration from a 15th century French manuscript

So there is really substantial evidence in the Biblical story itself. For Jonah, in his three-day experience of the Underworld, is testifying that he was descending into a murky gloomy realm, in fact the Realm of the Dead. And in fact amongst the early Christians, living under persecution in the Roman Catacombs, some paintings have survived from the 3rd century, that depict this incident. from this esoteric, hidden aspect. But very interestingly, the whale is shown as a kind of spirit monster; and this just is how the Netherworld was thought of in ancient times, see illustration 2.

There are few other references to this three-day process in Hebrew literature. A brief passage in a later Hebrew prophet, called Hosea is interesting. He refers to a central theme in this process, that the inner spiritual help coming from a high spiritual source, is usually called 'the Lord' in Hebrew literature. But at one point he mentions a three-day process which finishes in a resurrection, and it appears to be an allusion to either the coming of a Messiah or else it refers to the personal initiatory process. Since these two are symbiotically linked, the lack of clarity here is perhaps to be expected,

> "After two days will he revive us; in the third day he
> will raise us up, and we shall live in his sight"
> (Hosea 6:2, NJKV version)

This sentence is an enigma to commentators; it just doesn't fit the usual message of such a writer, nor the context of the chapter he is writing. It appears to be a veiled reference to the initiatory process. Since the actual procedures involving the initiatory process were kept totally confidential, it is little wonder that written evidence for them is hard to find. But there is a special text from the Hellenistic Age, written in Greek, which appears to have it origins in initiatory Hebrew circles, called the Odes of Solomon. They survive today only in a Syriac version.

The Odes of Solomon are in the form of poems of praise to the Divine (called 'the Lord'), in the manner of the Psalms. To give a date for this text is difficult, and scholars differ, but we conclude that it was written about 100 BC, but later became subject to some editorial activity, early in the Christian era. Three of the 42 odes do have a definite reference to Christ, but it is likely that this name was inserted in a later century by a Christian editor.

Although today they are admired in some religious circles for their general piety, their underlying initiatory message is not perceived. What is so significant about this collection of odes is that they contain veiled indications about the three-day initiatory process of the Mysteries. These odes indicate, like the story of Jonah, that in Hebrew religious-spiritual circles the general nature of the three-day initiatory 'sleep', and the consequent experiences of the Underworld, were well known.

The initiatory Odes to Solomon

An examination of how the ancients communicated their initiatory teachings shows that they would write a document in a way which had two meanings; a public, obvious meaning and a hidden, cryptic meaning. When an initiatory meaning is to be communicated in a religious verse it is veiled beneath another layer of meaning, which also reads perfectly well to the non-initiated. The narrator or the main character in the verse can actually change identity mid-stream; from an acolyte to a spirit being of some kind. Following are some extracts from these odes:

> Ode 42
> I stretched out my hands and approached my Lord, for the spreading out of my hands is His sign. And my extension is the upright wood, that was lifted up on the way of the Righteous One.... ... Sheol saw me and was shattered, and Death ejected me, and many with me. [39]

Here we leave behind the orthodox concepts of accepted Biblical texts, and enter the sphere of the initiatory striving in the Hellenistic world. The narrator recounts that, having been initiated in the Mysteries, he can, through the three-day sleep, ascend up into spirit realms and function consciously in his soul. This stage occurs after the descent down into the Underworld. We note also here the significant feature that the acolyte indicates that his arms are outstretched, as if he were in effect stretched out on a cross of wood. This seems to suggest that during the three-day process the acolyte could either be placed in a sarcophagus or placed on a wooden cross (perhaps lying flat on the ground). This indicated also in Ode 21,

---

[39] The Odes to Solomon, in The lost books of the Bible, edit. F. Crane, World Publishing Co., Cleveland, 1926 ; and Die Oden Salomos, trans. W. Bauer, KIT 1963.

Ode 21
My arms I lifted up to the Heights, to the grace of the Lord: because He had cast off my fetters from me: and my Helper had lifted me up to His grace and to His salvation. And I took off the darkness and clothed myself with light. And my soul acquired limbs free from illness, affliction or pain...

Here the text is clearly indicating an initiatory process. Being clothed with light is a way of saying to those with ears to hear, that one is having a kind of out-of-the-body experience. Before we leave these Odes and move on to the extraordinary secret parallelism between the Mysteries and the death of Christ, we shall consider a small extract from Ode 22.

This text indicates sophisticated spiritual experiences, and confirms that the initiatory process of descending into the Underworld, and later of encountering the divine, lies behind the entire composition. Here the narrator, who is deep in Sheol, may well be writing from a perspective of an inspiring spiritual being, active within the spiritual-soul of a human being,

"....They {spirit beings} who saw me, marvelled at me, because I was persecuted, and they supposed that I was swallowed up {disempowered in Hades}..."

And then some verses later, he writes of things so transcendent that they must remain an enigma. Namely, that in the Netherworld, this person (or avatar-like being) was not successfully attacked by malignant entities because 'the memory of the evil beings did not reach back to the point of origin of his own being';

"...And they sought for my death but did not attain it: for I was older than their memory reached. And vainly did they make attack upon me..."

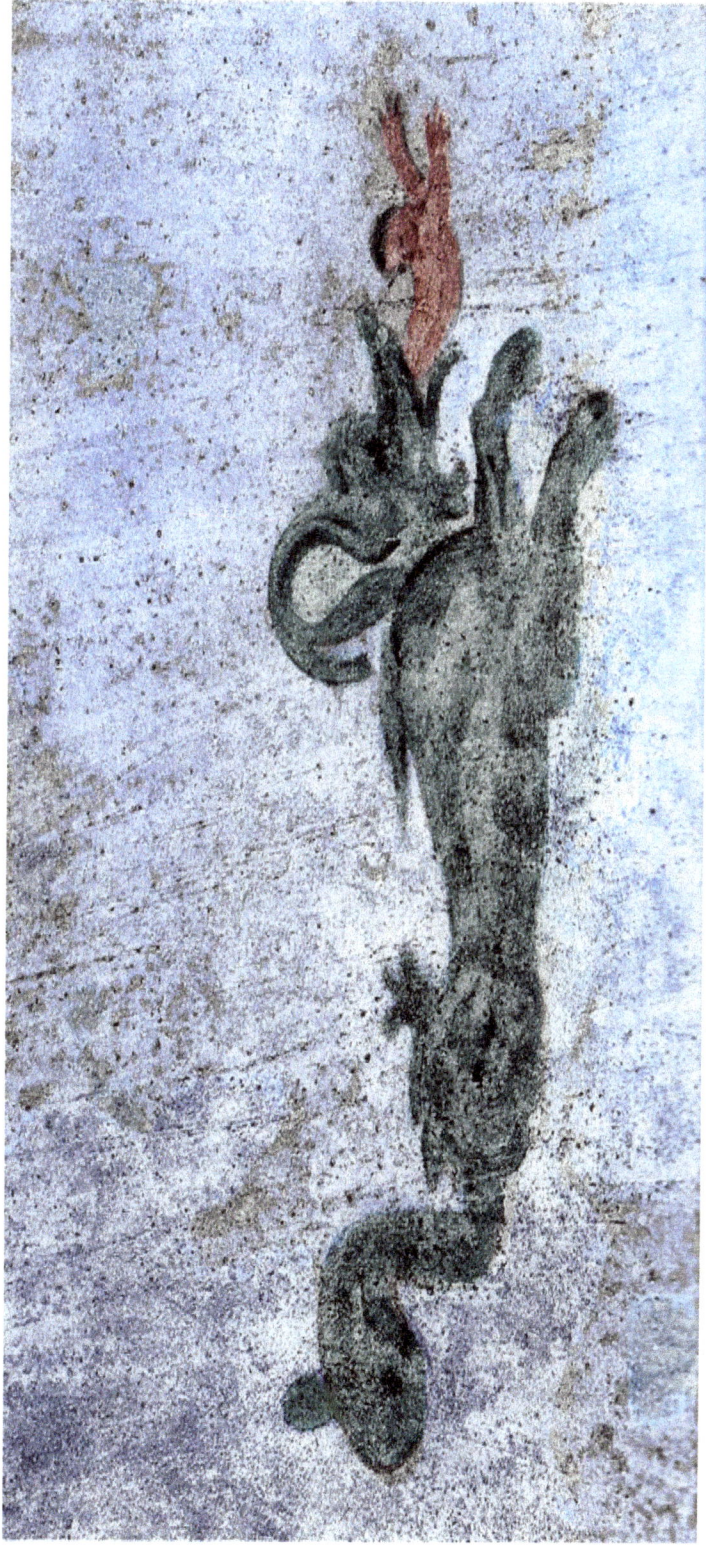

2   Jonah's "whale" as an aquatic monster ca. 280 AD in the Catacomb of Priscilla, Rome.
A symbol of the Netherworld, not a whale

(image slightly enhanced

This initiatory idea is repeated again, in Ode 28, in a different way; he was not attacked because 'his begetting was not like theirs'. Whatever we might like to make of this enigmatic verse, it becomes obvious that the text has an initiatory origin, and is basically about someone experiencing an initiatory interaction which involves spirit beings, in the Underworld. So, early in the first century AD, against a colourful background of the Greek and Egyptian Mysteries, of orthodox Judaism, and of discreet Hebrew Mysteries, the key events which lead to the forming of the Christian religion, the death of Jesus, took place.

The impact of Christianity on the Mysteries
Around AD 33 a new and spiritually dramatic event happened, an event which changed the religious landscape forever. A holy preacher, a miracle-worker from Galilee, was crucified, because of opposition to his radical teachings from key power figures in the Hebrew-Roman establishment of the time. But, during his short three years of ministry, many miracles were reported, involving remarkable healings, and even restoring life to those who had died. He left no written documents for posterity, but he gave the highest ethical-moral teachings in his parables and brief sermons. With his death it seemed that this person's brief, but deeply spiritual, interaction with people was now permanently over.

However – and this is the most striking feature of his life – setting it apart from the lives of other founders of religions, word began to spread three-days after his death, that he was resurrected, and was appearing to his disciples in a somewhat ethereal, but nevertheless tangible form. He was somehow resurrected from the death process, after three days. It was these extraordinary reports which above all else, actually brought about the impetus amongst the people of Palestine and elsewhere to create a new religion, originally known as "the Way".

More and more people concluded that this preacher, Jesus of Nazareth, had in some manner overcome death – that he was being experienced by surprised and awed followers as a fully conscious, and highly sanctified person, although not existing in the normal flesh body. And those who believed this, concluded that his resurrection implied some kind of extremely important alteration for the better in the after-death state of human beings, and also in humanity's over-all future destiny.

Despite the improbability of this, the people who experienced him, or who heard about this from others, concluded that he had indeed dealt in some way triumphantly with the death process. It was in fact these reports that brought about the creation of the new religion. (The fact that it was women who first saw him is a potent sociological fact.[40]) Very significantly, these reports about Jesus reappearing after his death, meant something really startling to the Hellenistic people.

For he was thereby presenting a solution to precisely the primary spiritual crisis of the people of his Age – the fear of being extinguished after death ! As we noted earlier, the fear of death arose for the first time in this Age, and became the widespread anxiety with people throughout the entire Hellenistic world. Only when a clear grasp is attained of the changes occurring in human consciousness over the ages can we rightly appreciate these, or any other, major dynamics. It is vital to see that before this new and remarkable story of the surviving of death by Jesus with its large, if not fully defined, implications, there was only one group of people who could claim triumph over death in some way – **those who had been initiated in the Mysteries** !

The reports about this person, Jesus of Nazareth, whom his disciples regarded as the anticipated Messiah, soon began to spread throughout the Hellenistic world. Dedicated missionaries began the dangerous task of bringing the message to the people of their era. It was not long before many ordinary people came to the conclusion, that they too could have the possibility, after death, of avoiding becoming virtually extinguished in the dreary Sheol or Hades, because of something that had occurred during this three-day process. And this applied to anyone, whether poor, or women or slaves; it was not restricted to upper class males, and it did not require the three-day sleep, nor did it require a momentous out-of-the-body encounter with higher worlds.

Now, this was a striking societal fact, namely that which was previously restricted to initiates of the Mysteries who underwent the three-day process, was now, in a different way, being announced as accessible to ordinary people. Instead of the probationary time and arduous trials, the Christian was asked to

---

[40] There are implications of this, including that it is saying to the reader of the New Testament that women are, in the mind of Jesus (or of the Gospel writers if you wish) of equal importance to men – and this in a culture where women were treated as inferior!

acknowledge their lower self (referred to as the sinful nature) and to confirm their intention to rise above this through their adherence to the teachings of Christ. This lead to the practice in Christianity of the 'confessing of sins'. A few decades later, as people in the Hellenistic world read the four main gospels about him, they were struck by the fact that his main promise to humanity whilst he was alive, had been directly relevant to this baffling, but sacred, phenomenon of him appearing after death.

He promised, as his major gift to people, to give them "eternal life" – a phrase which was understood to mean having an existence in the after-life. In the gospels a language was used which presented many sublime events and teachings, but the initiatory or 'esoteric' significance of these was not directly presented in such public texts.

There were other gospels which did present a directly esoteric viewpoint, these were discovered in the mid 20th century at Nag Hammadi in Egypt. However, the situation is complex. For recent research into the Greek texts of the Gospels in the Bible has revealed that an initiatory meaning **was also placed inside the biblical Scriptures themselves**. This meaning was hidden inside by the use of complex grammatical techniques. Now the promise made by Jesus to people about overcoming death, and his appearances to various people after his own death, must have been immensely moving to the people who became Christians in the decades after the initial events.

But this very same situation would have been really puzzling, even affronting, to those initiated in the Mysteries. They would have thought of this as quite mistaken, perhaps as fraud. Or they would have considered it to be something of intense sacredness, involving a kind of new, incisive spiritual dynamic occurring for humanity. As Rudolf Steiner taught, those who were initiated in the Mysteries were told that,

> .... in the future there would arise a person who would do something to enable all human beings, not just these chosen acolytes, to have the spark of the Christ-light enkindled in their soul. This someone was always in high spiritual realms, but instead of people all having to go out their body for a somewhat perilous three-day process, this 'someone' would bring the spiritual realms down into the earthly and human spheres.[41]

---

[41] From a lecture of 2nd Dec. 1096, in Cologne.

Indeed if these initiated person were attentive, they would have noted that the features reported about the Crucifixion and on to the time of the Resurrection had a striking parallelism with their own initiation process. We shall explore this intriguing parallelism in the next chapter further.

CHAPTER SIX: The Mysteries, the Sun God & secrets of Christianity

Parallelism between the Mysteries and the events on Golgotha hill

Jesus was condemned to death by the repulsive method of crucifixion. According to Rudolf Steiner and some early church authorities this occurred on Friday, April 3rd, in AD 33. Recent detailed astronomical studies into ancient Jewish calendar systems, have confirmed this date.[42] The evening before, together with his disciples, he had celebrated a Passover festival; this became known in Christianity as the Last Supper. But on this occasion, the strictly required roasted Lamb was not offered, not present on the table; this was to signify that Jesus himself would be sacrificed (the next day). After his arrest on Friday morning, after scourging and interrogation, he was taken to Golgotha hill just outside the walls of Jerusalem to be crucified.

At midday he was nailed to the cross and three hours later, at 3pm he was dead. That evening his body was taken down and placed in a tomb, where he lay throughout Saturday until Sunday, the third day. On Sunday morning, the gospels report that he was resurrected, that is he had risen from the dead, being seen by Mary Magdalene who went to the tomb to anoint his body for burial. Later he was seen by other disciples.

The events on Golgotha hill outside Jerusalem where Jesus was crucified, seem to form a parallel to the initiatory process, which required a three-day sleep. According to Rudolf Steiner this took place either in a sarcophagus, or by lying out-stretched upon a horizontal cross, before being spiritually re-born or 'resurrected'. In the Mysteries, the acolytes who underwent the three-day process were poetically considered dead, as they lay there. As we noted earlier, Rudolf Steiner taught that during this time the soul of the acolyte was helped by senior members of the Mystery centre to descend into the Underworld, and later in the process they ascended up into higher realms, to encounter their deity.

Then on the third day they were carefully awakened out of their special state, and felt themselves to be resurrected or 're-born

---

[42] The Mystery of the Last Supper, by Prof. Colin J Humphreys, Cambridge Univ. Press, 2011.

from on high', as the texts about the Mysteries indicate. So, this three-day process in the Mysteries has some similarities to the events that occurred on Golgotha hill.

Furthermore, during his ministry, Jesus was asked to give a kind of miraculous sign, to prove that he was the Messiah. He replied by saying that there would be only one sign given, and that was the 'the sign of Jonah'. (Matt. 16:4) Although this is no longer emphasized in Western churches today, it was firmly believed by the gospel writers and the first disciples, according to the earliest Christian documents, that during the three-days, as Jesus lay in the tomb, his soul descended into the Underworld, into the dreary, murky oceanic Sheol or Hades realm. St. Matthew states,

> For as Jonah was three days and three nights in the belly of a huge fish, so the Son of Man will be three days and three nights in the heart of the earth.

This concept of Jesus being placed in a kind of replica to the three-day experience of the Mysteries is referred to a number of times in the New Testament. St. Paul refers to this theme in Romans (10:7); "...who shall descend into the Abyss {to bring Christ back up}? There is also a supportive reference in Ephesians (4:9); "...he descended into the lower parts of the Earth" and another in Philippians (2:10); "...every knee should bend at the name of Jesus, those in heaven, those on the earth, and those *under* the earth."

It is also in the testimony of the first century Bishop, Papias, who reported that the first Elders of the Church taught the descent of the Christ into Hades. As we saw earlier, this is just what Jonah did, and probably thousands of other persons too, who over the millennia were initiated.

This realm of the Dead, in its lowest, most sinister aspects, was believed to exist far below the Earth's surface, but not in a physical sense. This concept of Jesus descending into this realm was quite well known in medieval times, often being depicted. Careful investigation of the Greek text of the Christian Scriptures has shown this in fact to be an integral part of the earliest Christian beliefs. It is not a superstitious legend placed on the scriptures in some later centuries.

For it is actually in the first Epistle of Peter, that we find, in the Greek original, the most emphatic declaration of this process of a descent into the oceanic Hades realm (1Peter 4:5-6). In the New International Version it simply reads as follows:

> But they will have to give account to him who is ready to judge the living and the Dead. For this is the reason the gospel was preached even to who those who are **now** dead, so that they might be judged according to men in regard to the body, but live according to God in regard to the spirit. (author's emphasis)

Now, the above text is not startling; it simply says that before he died, Jesus preached to some people, people who died not so long after they heard Jesus. They were presumably elderly folk. But in fact, so startlingly esoteric is this passage in the original Greek, that, in accordance with the humanistic theological approach to this religion, modern translations actually alter the Greek to avoid presenting the original meaning as it is written in Greek. (!) In the New International Version (NIV) translation, an additional Greek word, which means 'now', is artificially added by the translators, to allow the initiatory implication to be dismissed.

This allows the passage to say that Jesus also preached to some people who are now dead, who had died before Peter wrote his epistle. Theologians generally comment that there is no authoritative report in the New Testament of such a descent by Jesus into the murky Hades realm. They conclude that this idea comes from a later series of texts, by people who didn't have a correct view of the mission of Jesus, (or perhaps too influenced by the 'katabasis' of the Mysteries).

But this attitude which dismisses the idea is itself incorrect. The NIV editors are entirely upfront about this alteration to the text, it is clearly stated that this is done. So, whereas the original text actually states that Jesus, at some point during the three-day process, descended spiritually into the Hades realm, the passage appears to be saying in the mainstream translations, that Jesus, prior to his arrest, had preached the gospel to various persons.

That is, to people who had died after Jesus' own death, but before this epistle was written by St. Peter. This is a much more comfortable view, but in fact the epistle is reporting on a process which, in some ways, is a very specific parallel to the Mysteries. A correct translation, where one refrains from inserting the word, 'now' is:

...they shall give an account to the One having readiness to judge living persons and dead persons. For this is the reason the gospel was also preached to dead persons {in Hades}, that they may be judged indeed as to the flesh, according to human nature, but {that} they may live as to the spirit, according to God."   (translation A. Anderson)

In other words, Christ preached to the dead, during the three-days to allow his message to reach not only living people but also the dead (i.e., the no longer incarnate) souls ! The theme of Christ's descent into Hades is also directly, but discreetly, found in the book of Hebrews (13:20); "...the God of peace, the one having brought up from the Dead the great Shepherd of the sheep..." The Shepherd is Jesus Christ, who was brought up out the Netherworld by God.

The events occurring over thee-days on Golgotha hill form a parallel to the experience of Jonah, in so far as there are three calendar days between the time when he was crucified, and when he was resurrected and appeared to Mary Magdalene. Therefore the events of Golgotha also a form a parallel – up to a point - of the initiatory process of the Mysteries. We noted that the story of Jonah was in effect about the descent into the Underworld.

The theological implications of this subject, and the entire complex features of the Greek grammar involved, cannot be dealt with here. But as we have seen, every New Testament writer has passages affirming this report made by St. Peter (although much less so with St. John). Thus this theme is not a later invention by people who did not understand the facts, and added some fanciful details. On the contrary, it is in fact a primary aspect of the deeds of the Messiah, and understood by his first disciples, and stated in the gospels or epistles. As such, it is a matter which is closely linked to the kind of experiences undergone in the initiatory process of the ancient Mysteries.

Naturally, to the modern Christian, this idea is unacceptable; and for several reasons. In particular they would ask, why would the Saviour need to be initiated ? He would not need that ! And this objection is completely valid. The point here is that what occurred on Golgotha hill was not another personal initiation, such as the Mysteries offered for millennia. It was a **cosmic equivalent** to the personal initiation process; it brought about the union of the planet Earth – and hence humanity – with the divine. But the events occurring on Golgotha hill did involve some elements – as we have already noted – that were similar to those of the Mysteries. We shall be able to see more clearly the cosmic nature of these events once we have unveiled the profound dynamics being hinted at in the gospels.

The Cry from the Cross, forsaken or glorified?
Further statements exist in early Christian documents which provide additional evidence of a startling parallelism between the events of the Crucifixion and Resurrection, and the initiatory process offered in the Mysteries. At this point there is the strange fact that it is reported of Jesus that, whilst on the cross, he called out in distress shortly before he dies, that he was forsaken by God. The words that he spoke are given in the gospels firstly in an Aramaic-Hebrew mixture and then translated by the gospel writer himself into Greek. This is how it appears in the NIV Bible in Matthew's Gospel 27:46,

> "He cried out, "Eloi, Eloi, lama sabachthani?"— which means, "My God, my God, why have you forsaken me?"

It is the word, 'forsake' (written by Matthew as 'sabachthani'), which is difficult to understand. Over the centuries it has been often rejected as an error by the church. Yet it has also been accepted by other Christians very reluctantly, that this statement is correct, even though it is hard to reconcile with the general sense of a mission which was undertaken, and which was proclaimed later as a success.

Many efforts have been made from the early centuries of Christianity onwards to remove these words or to somehow get around the implication of these words (such as by changing the Greek text in very old papyrus copies of the scriptures). Christian belief is that such a sacrificial death by Jesus was in fact a predestined part of a sublime process, and this does not actually harmonize with an exclamation of great despair. One reason that the text as it stands is accepted to some extent, is that it is linked to Psalm 22, where similar feelings are expressed by king David,

> My God, my God, why have you forsaken me? Why are you so far from saving me, so far from the words of my groaning? O my God, I cry out by day, but you do not answer, by night {also}, and {thus I} am not silent.

People also very understandably concluded that the key word 'sabachthani' must mean 'to forsake', because the Greek gospels themselves give the meaning of these words (whether written in Aramaic or Hebrew) in a Greek translation, which in English reads, "My god, my god, why hast thou forsaken me?" In other words, the word 'sabachthani' is presented in the gospels as a way of translating a Semitic word for 'forsake' into Greek. So the scholars' assumptions here that it does mean 'forsake' are of course, quite reasonable.

But still many Christians have been left wondering just why this cry of despair was recorded, suggesting as it does, a feeling of failure or at least huge inner turmoil. People have thought, "Well, I guess it must have been said, but if it was, why then record it? Surely that is a bit odd?" So, let's examine what might be going on here. Are there other indications in the gospel passage that some kind of initiatory 'mystery' took place on Golgotha, perhaps on a great scale, yet nevertheless a replica of the Mysteries? We have already seen that there was the three-day time scale, and there was a descent into Hades; both of these are part of the old Mysteries.

Firstly, see how the reports of this incident moves from one language to another:

Matthew 27:46 =	"Eli, Eli,	lema	sabachthani"
	Hebrew	Aramaic	Aramaic
Mark 15:34 =	"Eloi, Eloi,	lama	sabachthani"
	Aramaic	Hebrew	Aramaic

We note also that Mark has "Eloi, Eloi", whereas Matthew has "Eli, Eli". The word 'Eli' is Hebrew for 'why?' and is given as such in Matthew. But 'Eloi' is an unknown word, a riddle; it is thought that perhaps it is a garbled rendering of Aramaic for 'why' (which however properly is, 'elahi'). So right here is a strange enigma.

But why would one writer give Hebrew and the other give a garbled Aramaic version? But the next word, 'lema', as given in Matthew is Aramaic and means approximately 'why' in Aramaic; so it is Matthew who is now giving the Aramaic. Then in Mark we find a different word, 'lama', which is Hebrew; so this time it is Mark who gives the Hebrew! This version with 'lama' is found in 10 major ancient manuscripts, and significantly these include very reliable ancient texts.[43]

---

[43] Such as Codex B, the 'Vaticanus', (4th cent.) and Codex D, the 'Cantabrigiensis', 5th century.

But, there are various other versions of this word to be found in ancient manuscripts of the New Testament. There is the word 'lima' (recorded in ancient 18 versions), and also the word 'leima'; these are all understood to be garbled versions of one or the other word. So, something very odd is going on here. In modern times scholars 'smoothed out' these differences to create a uniform Greek text, and settled on their choice of 'lema'. This was a reasonable decision, as it appears to be the most accurate version. But the point is that these many versions exist, indicating a strange confusion prevailed long ago. Unfortunately the smoothing out of the confusion is itself a misleading action.

Why is this misleading? Just consider the key word, 'sabachthani'. You will find writers and learned scholars stating in authoritative books, that this Semitic word, sabachthani, "is an Aramaic word". However, this statement is **not actually correct**. It is indeed a composition of Aramaic letters (represented in Greek), but it is **not** an Aramaic word ! Rather, it is a garbled group of letters from this language. The distinction is important !

Because knowing this, a spiritually alert scholar has to determine to what actual Aramaic word this group of letters might refer; but without any context, it has no known meaning. That is, if the gospel writer himself had not gone on to give a translation into Greek, we would really be in the dark about it. For there would be several words which one could reasonably assume it means.

Now, an examination of the ancient papyri and codices show that variations existed with this word in the gospels too, e.g., some ancient versions of the gospel have sibakthanei, or zabafthanei, or sabaxthanei. None of these are true Aramaic words (presented in a Greek form). So they are all garbled forms of an Aramaic text, as indeed a few precise scholars do acknowledge.[44] Now scholars have concluded that these various Greek terms, which are all 'smoothed out' to read 'sabachthani' in any standard Greek-English New Testament, is in fact a rendering of the verb, Shebaq, to forsake, (in this sentence,

---

[44] Ulrich Lux, Das Evangelium nach Matthäus (Mt 26-28), Evangelisch-Katholischer Kommentar zum Neuen Testament, S. 332; and A. T. Robertson, A Greek Grammar of the New Testament, Broadman Press, Nashville, 1934, p. 463; and D. Wallace, Greek Grammar beyond the basics, Zondervan, Grand Rapids, 1996, p. 59.

Shebaq-tani = you have forsaken). They assume this is the right conclusion because after all, the gospel report goes on to say that it means to forsake !

But the reason that we are exploring this very theme, and therefore questioning whether it does mean 'to forsake' or not, is that just **this kind of uncertainty can be an indicator of a secret initiatory meaning**, placed in the original documents. In other words, the confusing, complex situation here may well be deliberate.

In fact, there is recent tradition in mystical groups of the western world that this passage in the gospels does indeed have another meaning. It is believed that it is presenting in a veiled way the initiatory meaning, 'to glorify', not to forsake. In 1875 an American esotericist, J. R. Skinner, whose ideas greatly influenced many Theosophists, declared in a book, in which he argued directly from the Hebrew text given in the gospel, that this sentence really means, "My God, my God, how thou hast glorified me!"[45] He doesn't go into the linguistic facts to academically prove his statement, however.

There are probably two reasons for him declaring this. One is that anyone who knows the Hebrew language can in fact decide that the strange non-word in the Gospel does most likely mean 'to glorify' (we shall examine why this is, below). The other reason is, that Skinner was a Freemason, and through this organisation was informed no doubt about the triumphant exclamation made by an acolyte in the initiation process (we shall explore this point, too). Certainly Jesus was not an acolyte, but the inspired way the gospels were written specifically intends to hint at a parallel.

The other person who taught that the sentence means 'to be glorified', not 'forsaken', is Rudolf Steiner. He taught that in the ancient Mysteries, as the acolyte arose from the three-day initiation sleep in ancient Egypt, the cry was heard "my God, my God, how thou hast glorified me!" It was made by the acolyte as they awoke, or by the hierophant. Steiner's perspective on the New Testament account of the words on the cross came from several sources. One source was his own knowledge, achieved through his seership, of what happened in the ancient Mysteries. Another was that Rudolf Steiner had his own direct perception of the life of Christ, allowing him to conduct this

---

[45] Skinner, "The Key to the Hebrew-Egyptian Mystery in the Source of Measures.

spiritual research. He lectured specifically on many truths in the life of Jesus, whether recorded in the Gospels in a veiled way, or not presented in the Bible.

However it appears that no scholarly linguistic work has been carried out to give concrete textual basis to this conclusion. There are apparently no theologians who argue for the word 'glorified'. For example, in 1963 a theologian published a very learnéd and detailed analysis of the words of Jesus from the cross. But he did not even discuss the word 'sabachthani' at all, let alone note that this word is not really a Greek form of 'sabachthani', and thus could have another meaning than 'forsaken'. (!)[46]

Whilst a much more recent, excellent commentary, on just the last two chapters alone of St. Matthew's gospel (480 pages in length) also omits any discussion of this topic.[47] But there are theologians who point out that in St. John's Gospel, Jesus does refer to a glorifying of his own being as a result of his imminent death on Golgotha.

Therefore, the cry from the cross could theologically be viewed as a kind of prelude to a glorification. It is the case too, that at the end of Psalm 22, there is the triumphant cry about future generations declaring that the Lord has completed his saving work for humanity. So theologians accept the idea of 'forsaken' by noting that the Psalm, and Christian theology, both point to a positive future, a glorification (of humanity, and of Jesus, respectively). So we will now look at the linguistics to see what basis there may be for this alternative view, namely, that it means 'glorified'.

Was Jesus 'forsaken' or was he 'glorified'?
This alternative view, that the sentence is referring to him being glorified, does in fact have a basis, linguistically. For there is another verb in Aramaic which these various muddled words could equally well be representing. This other verb is Shabah-tani **and it means, 'to glorify'.** (Remember, the other word was Shebaq-tani, to forsake.) Despite the fact that the meanings of these two verbs are so very different, you can see that they are spelt in a very similar way. So therefore anyone who knows the

---

[46] Thorleif Boman, *Das Letzte Worte Jesu*, in Studia Theologica; Nordic Journal of Theology VOL 17, issue 2, 1963.
[47] Ulrich Lux, Das Evangelium nach Matthäus (Mt 26-28), Evangelisch-Katholischer Kommentar zum Neuen Testament, S. 332.

Aramaic language may indeed very validly conclude that the expression 'Eli, Eli, lema sabachthani' and its various versions, actually means, 'My god, my god, how thou hast *glorified* me!'

It is important to note again that the strange mixture, in Greek, 'sabachthani', does not represent the Aramaic verb 'to forsake'. An odd interchanging of letters between the two languages has to be carried out for this translation to occur. The word 'sabachthani' could, with this same type of rough interchange, also be traced back to the verb 'to glorify'. However, in fact it is much nearer to the Aramaic word 'glorify' than it is to the word 'forsake'.[48] So, linguistically, this word in fact could be either to forsake or to glorify, **but is much more likely to mean to glorify**. In addition, there is the very supportive fact that the rest of the sentence is a deliberate muddle, too.

A Hierophantic phrase hidden inside the gospel narrative
The other confused elements of the text, such as the changing between Aramaic and Hebrew, tends to reinforce the conclusion to the meditant, that the text has a second layer of meaning. Perhaps an especially sacred meaning, which has some relationship to the Mysteries, is being given here. Is there any further evidence that reinforces this idea? Yes, there is. The Greek translation of some of the above, in Matthew's gospel, is itself a strange mixture of Hellenistic and Classic Greek. Classical Greek goes back centuries before Hellenistic Greek, almost to the dawn of Greek civilization, around 750 BC. It is the language of Greek Classical Greek writers, like Homer, Aristotle, and Plato. The New Testament is written in a common form of the later Hellenistic Greek.

Most of the comments we have about the Mysteries are in Classical Greek, as these were established at the beginning of Greek civilization (or even before it, by other peoples, and then assimilated by the Greeks). So, by the time of Christ, many centuries had passed by wherein the cry of the hierophant resounded from the sacred sites, as this official supervised the initiation experience. At some point in the process there would be perhaps a stern admonition, but at other times a jubilant cry, especially when the great three-day sleep was successfully over,

---

[48] For example, the Greek letter 'sigma' (σ) has to be stand in for the Aramaic shin (שׁ) and the Greek letter chi (χ) has to stand in for the Aramaic letter Qof (ק); neither of these exchanges is really appropriate.)

(the 'Jonah' process). In such a jubilant cry, the god of that particular Mystery centre was given thanks.

This venerated tradition caused the old Classical Greek language to be retained even into the Hellenistic period, which is when Christ lived, and it was used especially when invoking a deity. For example, a Christian writer from the second century AD reports that in the Mysteries of Eleusis, a loud triumphant cry resounded from the guiding hierophant at the crucial moment of initiation,

> "Noble Brimo has begotten the holy boy, Brimos {her son} !
> The strong {goddess} has brought forth the strong!" [49]

The name Brimo was a name used for the goddess Demeter (and associated goddesses at Eleusis), and implies that she was a mighty goddess who inspired holy dread, in the sense of a deep feeling of awe. Brimos, as the name of her son, is not really a name, but is a term similar to her special name (i.e., it was an appellation). This is a way of saying that he was like unto her. So, in a loud triumphant cry, the hierophant is announcing that the great Earth goddess, Demeter, has brought to birth in an initiate the higher self, and that this higher self is symbiotically linked to the goddess. Now you can imagine that an acolyte undergoing this experience, in Greece or long ago in Egypt in a pyramidal chamber, would call out, or hear the call of the hierophant on their behalf; "My deity (Demeter, Osiris, etc), oh, how you have glorified (or blessed or perfected) me!

Now, all this is really important, because it reveals a subtle clue in the gospels that there is an initiatory message hidden in the report. We would have to ignore the very striking material we have explored above, about the deliberately confused linguistics to accept the report that Jesus in despair, cries out "My God, my God, why hast thou forsaken me? But in fact, we cannot ignore the strange linguistic problems, and we cannot ignore the strange mix of old Attic and contemporary Hellenistic Greek which is used here. We just have to query this strangely tragic exclamation.

You see, Jesus always referred to God as 'the Father'; so God was indeed 'God', not one of the many lesser gods of the Hellenistic world. And thus God was not 'a god', he was **the** God. This distinction between the Father-God and any other deity,

---

[49] The Mystery religions, S. Angus, Dover, N.Y. 1975, p.140.

when Jesus is speaking, is clearly marked in the Greek language. Now, although you cannot know this from a translation, or from a basic knowledge of Greek, when Matthew translates this strange muddled Aramaic-Hebrew sentence, and says that it states, "My God, my God, why hast thou forsaken me?", he actually uses in his translation, an old Attic Greek term **used in the secret sanctuary of the Mysteries**!

That is, one would expect that Jesus' words in Greek, when addressing God would be, "*Ho theos mou, theos mou*",[50] and in fact he does say this in Mark's report. This term, ho theos, is the normal way of Jesus or any one else in those times, addressing God. But in Matthew's account, he says, "*the-e mou, the-e mou*".[51] This is in fact ancient Attic Greek, and is the very term used in the Mysteries, when invoking or praising a spiritual being, a deity !!

To see this startling fact more clearly, we need to know that there was in existence long before Matthew wrote his gospel, a Greek translation of the Jewish scriptures (the 'Old Testament'); these were originally written in Hebrew. This translation, called the Septuagint, was made to help those Hellenistic Jews who did not speak Hebrew any more. Gospel writers quite often quote from the Septuagint, as it has made the Old Testament understandable to Greek-speaking Jews.

But as Professor Ulrich Lux points out, here the gospel writer alters the Greek version of the Septuagint in his quote. He changes it, so that he has Jesus addressing what we assume to be 'God', with this Attic Greek word.[52] This is the only place in the New Testament were it is to be found, it occurs nowhere else in the New Testament. So, it implies that here Jesus is speaking to a spirit-being or a particular god of some religion (or Mystery cult), **and not the Father-God** ! Or that the esoterically alert reader could be informed that a variation of the initiation process well-known in the Mysteries, has occurred.

Now this use of language is a bit subtle, so the normal reader in the Hellenistic world would assume that the Father-God is being appealed to by Jesus. But for those involved with the Mysteries,

---

[50] that is = ʹΟ θεος μου, ʹΟ θεος μου

[51] that is = Θεέ μου, Θεέ μου

[52] Ulrich Lux, Das Evangelium nach Matthäus (Mt 26-28), Evangelisch-Katholischer Kommentar zum Neuen Testament, S. 332.

the implication of having the ancient Attic Greek term, is nothing less than an initiation has occurred !

The cry from the cross and Eleusis

Now, summing up, since we have seen that this sentence can mean 'to glorify' or 'to forsake', we can look at this strange sentence as being similar to that used in the Mysteries when a deity is being addressed during an initiation process ! So on the cross, Jesus, just in the moment before his death, calls out the great clarion call of the Hierophant in the Mysteries:

"My deity! My deity! How thou hast glorified me !

Rudolf Steiner taught, whenever an acolyte arose from the three-day sleep, they were greeted with this sacred exclamation.[53] As Rudolf Steiner's teachings make clear, this is a declaration which is true of Jesus, because as a result of this deed, he arises out of his body into the heights of divine realms, (called 'Devachan' in anthroposophy). But furthermore, in this process Jesus becomes eternally linked to a divine being (a process which we shall explore later in this book.) So this age-old hierophantic call, which directly alludes to the pivotal event in the Mysteries is true, but in a new way, of Jesus.

This sentence, in the way that it has been so specially formulated in the gospels, parallels the most potent experience of the acolyte in the Mysteries when he or she was initiated. It evokes the moment when the hierophant called out a cry of holy jubilation to the effect that the acolyte had been glorified by their god, by immersion in the spiritual realms. They now had their higher self born within them (they did not stay in the lower soul realms for the entire time, but ascended up into divine realms). The confusion in the Gospel texts is due to the need to keep the deeper meaning veiled.[54]

Now there are other hidden indications of a secret being veiled here, a secret that would puzzle modern Christians, and requires initiatory insight to unveil. To discover this additional indication, we need to note that in the Septuagint there is of course a Greek translation of the Psalms, as these are part of the Old Testament, too. We noted earlier that the words of Jesus

---

[53] Given in a lecture from 5th. Nov. 1906.
[54] Rudolf Steiner indicated that these sacred realities would not be unveiled until the 20th century, as a help to a spiritual need.

on the cross, given in the two gospels, come from Psalm 22. Now the Hebrew text of this Psalm, as written in the Bible, starts with;

> My God, my God, why have you forsaken me? Why are you so far from saving me, so far from the words of my groaning?

But in the Septuagint, the Greek translators of the Hebrew added an extra phrase, to make the pathos of feeling defeated and rejected, even stronger: [55]

> My God, my God, draw near, hear me, why have you forsaken me? Why are you so far from saving me, so far from the words of my transgression...? [56]

Now, although both Mark and Matthew do quote the Septuagint in their translation of this sentence, they actually omit this extra part. And in doing this, they reduce the nuance of despair and of impending doom – **and thereby allow more space for the feeling of exultation**! And then, as we saw, Matthew especially makes use of an Attic phrase for invoking a deity. So, hidden in the text, for those who 'have eyes to see' are a number of grammatical devices which allow the gospel writers to indicate that there are parallels between the events of Golgotha, and the initiatory process of the Mysteries.

So what does it all mean? It means that, when read on the secret initiatory level, Jesus calls out a triumphant cry of praise and jubilation ! Not a cry of despair and doubt. The reason for the triumphant call has to do with a sense of the imminent triumph of the divine, in a great process which required of Jesus a 'katabasis', a descent into Sheol or the lower Soul World. We shall see something of what this great process is, as we factor in the role of the sun spirit, and finalize our exploration of this new religion from the perspective of the Mysteries.

But for many Christians at this point there will be another question arising here: how could it be possible that a gospel text has **two** meanings in it? Surely the gospels are straightforward, and written for the benefit of every person, including the uneducated. And what interest would a true Christian have with hidden mystical matters, like initiatory practises – surely that

---

[55] Septuaginta editit Alfed Rahlfs, edit. 6. Stuttgart, Privilegierte Württembergische Bibelanstalt, Psalmi 21, Vol 2, p. 19.
[56] The Greek expression here for 'draw near, hear me' can also be translated as 'heed me, tend to me'.

was not part of this new, wholesome religion? The response here has to be that these objections are the result of a superficial, humanistic approach to the Bible. Academic research by this author has established that the Greek text does have these two layers of meaning.[57]

Part of the difficulty in accepting these discoveries lies in the fact that it is a culturally conditioned view of Christianity from its very outset that this religion, had no link whatsoever to initiatory spirituality. And certainly nothing to do with ancient pagan Mysteries ! Unfortunately this shallow viewpoint has become deeply ingrained. This situation has an historical basis in the battle that the early church fathers fought against Gnostic spirituality, which had accepted a wide range of spirit beliefs, but could not accept the unique message of the new religion.

As we have just seen, the most sacred core event which created the Christian religion – the events on Golgotha hill – has three deliberate parallels to the act of initiation in the Mysteries. One is the sign of Jonah – when Jesus had three days existing in a death-like condition. A second parallel occurs when he is described as descending into the Underworld and interacting with spirits there, which was a central focal point of the initiatory process.

The third parallel is the great cry of exultation of Jesus on the cross, so similar to the exulting cry of the hierophant in the Mysteries. Strange as this may sound to Biblical scholars, complex and deliberate grammatical processes were actually undertaken by the gospel writers to both reveal and conceal such initiatory secrets in the text.

A Christian text in Initiatory Critical Analysis: a new text analysis tool

Since the 1850's various excellent text assessment tools (called literary 'criticisms') have been developed to help scholars gain a clearer understanding of a religious text. These tools or techniques consider the grammatical structure, the subtle editorial work done by the writer, the sources used in preparing a text, any associated traditions underlying how a story is formulated, the socio-political background or intentions. And these tools are important as they allow the majority of

---

[57] That is, quite apart from being susceptible to allegorical interpretations, discussed by earlier mystical Christians.

Christians to have a clearer understanding of the normal, non-esoteric meanings of the texts. However, this author has pioneered, in academic studies, a new 'pathway' to engaging with the text, with the special ability of discovering any initiatory meanings hidden in the text.

This could be called the Initiatory Intention approach (technically the 'Initiatory Critical Analysis'). With this tool, a contemplative working with the text is undertaken, in close association with the grammatical approach. With regard to just how the gospel writers expected their text to be received, if we leave out this new 'initiatory assessment' then many passages in the New Testament often remain baffling. No meaningful explanation is forthcoming about them from theologians. But when the Initiatory Critical Analysis is applied, for example in this passage, then we realize that the confused variety of terms was used in order to give an indication that within this confused text there lies a sacred secret.[58]

In the early centuries of Christianity, this strange mixture could lead those who were aware of the great cry of jubilation made in the Mysteries when the acolyte was resurrected, to contemplate the gospel account of the events on Golgotha on a mystical level. They would realize that it also has the meaning of 'to glorify'.

But generally other people, who were not aware of these esoteric things, (and they would outnumber the first group greatly), would relate to the surface translation given by the gospel writer, and understand this to refer to the pain and suffering made in sacrifice by Jesus, and think of it as simply meaning 'to forsake'. The Christian religion was founded during the period of the decay of the Mysteries, and then it became consolidated during the development of an increasingly limited, non-holistic attitude, which characterizes the western world. Consequently, **it carries within itself an impediment to recognizing the initiatory teachings, subtly woven into its own texts.** But it started out as a religion that had an initiatory core, and a specific parallelism with the Mysteries.

Although it offered a parallel initiatory path to that of the Mysteries, its path was no doubt different in various ways, for it

---

[58] The full implication of this new exegetical tool cannot be elucidated here, but scholars will note that the understanding of the 'Sitz-Im-Leben' critical assessment path of a Biblical text also needs to be revised.

offered a new approach to spirituality. There is quite an abundance of evidence of this in the very earliest Christian writings. In St. Paul's writings there are several references to 'mysteries', by which he means secrets of an initiatory kind. Of course, his use of the word, 'Mysteries', does not have to refer to precisely the same things that the same word means to a priest of the cult of Demeter. But it does indicate privileged higher knowledge, indications of this are to be found in early Christian writers.

CHAPTER SEVEN: Christianity once a religion with an initiatory core

Christian Mysteries: Ignatius, Clement and St. Paul

References to 'mysteries' occur in the writings of Ignatius, bishop of Antioch in Syria, written about 115 AD. He was very much in touch with beginnings of the movement. Some of the original followers of Christ may have still been alive when Ignatius was a young man, and certainly their students would have been known to him. In his writings he adopts the language of a person involved in the Greek Mysteries; such phrases as "you are fellow-initiates of Paul, he who became sanctified..." and in a later letter, "...it is necessary that those who are 'deacons' of the "Mysteries" of Jesus to..."[59]

One could conclude that such expressions are innocent of any nuance of the mystical secrets of actual initiation, and refer only to ecclesiastical matters, because the Christians first adopted, and then adapted, such words to their own use. On some occasions it appears that they may well be this, but certainly not always.

One recalls that St. Paul spoke about confidential mysteries, which he allows himself to only touch on in his public writings. He also spoke of being spiritually raised up, out of his body, in his soul, "into the **third** heaven".[60] This entry into spirit realms is precisely the type of experience that the Mysteries offered. And of course, this remark also establishes that to early Christians, as with the Mystery religions, there are a multiple of heavens, of ever higher states of glory, since Paul had a spiritual journey into the third one.

A further indication of the existence of initiatory knowledge and practices in early Christianity include the remarks from a prominent church father who was writing around 200 AD, Clement of Alexandria. Clement was the teacher of Origenes of Alexandria, whose brilliant insights and sincere spirituality made him a revered church father for centuries. Clement refers to the initiatory, somewhat Platonic nuances in St. Paul's writings, commenting that Plato had a true wisdom deriving from the Mysteries, and that there are 'esoteric' Christian truths

---

[59] In The Apostolic Fathers, Greek texts and English translations, edit. M. Holmes, Baker Books, Grand Rapids, 1992.
[60] 2Corinthians, 12:2

which are not to be divulged to the laity in general (esoteric means here restricted for those who are initiated). [61]

But it is intriguing that in regard to the new secret Christian mysteries, Clement writes that these are celebrated at night, "because the soul has withdrawn from the body then" (!) There is here obviously some parallel to what we learnt about the ancient three-day sleep process of the Mysteries of antiquity, because it involved the soul being withdrawn from the body which lay still for three-days. Clement goes onto say,

> "..after the baptism …comes the minor Mysteries, which have some instructional foundation and preliminary preparation for what is to come after these, and (especially) after the great Mysteries in which nothing remains to be learned, but to contemplate the universe…" [62]

The Secret gospel of St. Mark

Now, there is another indication of the existence of a deep link between the Mysteries and Christianity, in its earliest phase, from the discovery in a monastery in Israel of an extraordinary, ancient letter, written by Clement of Alexandria to an enquirer called Theodore. This letter actually mentions a secret gospel of St. Mark, "to be used only by those being initiated".

This private letter directly speaks of a system of seven degrees of initiation existing in the early church, and of a secret version of the gospel of St. Mark – an idea that was not acceptable to the modern church. It says in part,

> …Mark came over to Alexandria, bringing both his own notes and those of Peter, from which he transferred to his former book the things suitable to whatever makes progress towards knowledge. Thus he composed a more spiritual Gospel for the use of those being perfected. Nevertheless, he did not divulge the things not to be uttered, nor did he write down the hierophantic teachings. But to the stories already he added yet other s and moreover brought in certain sayings of which he knew the interpretation would, as a mystagogue, lead the

[61] Clement of Alexandria, Miscellanies, Book 5 Ante-Nicene Christian Library, Vol. 2, trans. W. Wilson, T & T Clark, Edinburgh, 1882, p 268.
[62] Clement of Alexandria, Miscellanies, Book 5 Ante-Nicene Christian Library, Vol. 2, trans. W. Wilson, T & T Clark, Edinburgh, 1882, p. 204.

hearers into the inner lost sanctuary of that truth hidden by seven veils...

We cannot go into the detailed theological dissension about this document here, but we note that many scholars rejected it. When one assesses their rejection it is clear that this is mainly because such an initiatory dimension to Christianity was naturally unacceptable, indeed incomprehensible to them. For example R. Gundry agreed with the conclusion that it was really a collection of mystical statements, put together from various sources, long after the lifetime of St. Mark.[63]

However such rejection from scholars occurred partly to distance themselves from a blasphemous misinterpretation which some people placed on the text by twisting its meaning. But as Charles W. Hedrick concludes in his detailed assessment of the theme, careful examination of the colour photos made of the document (the original letter being misplaced by the monks) indicate that it is an authentic discovery.[64] In addition, as soon as one is aware that the new religion came into being through a process which has parallels with an initiatory matters, then this fragment from the secret, initiatory gospel of St. Mark is correctly seen as a valid document. It is extremely important, for it appears that this religion itself will need a return to this kind of disciplined quest for entry into higher realms if it is to reclaim its position in society.

Now this same Clement in his books (called the Miscellanies of St. Clement) was quite open about the fact that after the initial baptism to become a Christian, there was a system of initiation into 'Mysteries'. These were obviously not the non-Christian Hebrew or Greek Mysteries, but some remodelled Christianized form of these. Clement was quite scathing of the superstitious nature of the traditional Greek Mysteries, many of which by now had become decadent. So, it is quite clear that some communities in the new religion of Christianity were involved in an esoteric mystical process, in short, in an initiatory process.

We now need to look at what is different about the events of Golgotha as compared to the initiatory process of the Mysteries.

---

[63] Robert Gundry, Mark: a Commentary on his Apology for the Cross, Eerdmans, 1993. Also F.F. Bruce, The Secret Gospel of Mark, Ethel M. Wood Lecture 11/Feb/1974, Univ. of London.
[64] For his article and other links, see
http://www.westarinstitute.org/Periodicals/4R_back_issues/SecretMk3/secretm k3.html

There is an intriguing indication hidden in the texts, of a major parallel between the age-old Mystery initiation process and the events on Golgotha hill. This is discovered when we examine the descent of the Saviour into the murky Underworld.

The first difference is of course, that in the age-old initiatory process a person was awakened or resurrected after three-days and had an illumined consciousness. But in the case of Jesus, his death ensued, so when it is said that he arose, resurrected, in a spiritualized form, it had a different sense to the old meaning of undergoing a katabasis.[65] The gospels give the alert reader the impression that something much more than a personal initiation was happening in those three-days. So what was this event ?

A different kind of descent to the Underworld

It is well-known that in antiquity the Underworld or realm of the dead was symbolically referred to as 'a murky sea', which correlates to the soul world. It was referred to in ancient Babylonia as the Apsu, in Greece it is Hades, and lies beneath the ocean. The finer part of the Netherworld consists of islands in the river of "deep swirling Okeanos" as Hesiod called it in *Works and Days*, an enormous river encompassing the world. This view of the Underworld is alluded to in a verse in the great Hymn to Demeter, dating from ca. 700 BC, from the Mysteries of Eleusis. It describes how after death an initiated person has a much better existence in the Underworld or realm of the dead, which is described as a 'murky gloom',

> Happy is he of men who has seen these things, but he who dies without fulfilling the holy things, and he has no share of them, has no claim ever on such blessings, when he is departed, down in the murky gloom... [66]

This way of referring to the realm of the dead, as a deep murky sea, was definitely still current in the first century AD, which is the era of the earliest Christian writings. This can be seen in *The Epistle of Barnabus*, written about AD 95. This Christian text, referring to the fate of evil souls after death, speaks of the Underworld as a murky sea,

---

[65] We cannot here explore the complex riddle behind the doctrine of the resurrection of the physical body, which refers not its flesh but to its archetypal structure (existing in an etheric and 'devachanic' form).
[66] In The Ancient Mysteries, edit. Marvin W. Myer, Univ. Pennsylvania, Philadelphia, 1999.

"{souls of such deceased men} with evil intentions.... move around just as fish do, in the darkness of the {'oceanic'} depths"... cursed, just as are cuttlefish, and (therefore have to} swim in the depths...in the mud." [67]
(translated the author)

Now, it is well-known that, in Christian understanding of the Bible, Christ is said to have died "in order to save people from their 'sinful nature" (i.e., the lower self). It is also said in Christian theology, based on a study of the gospels that, "he died on the cross because of our sinful nature". Now, the acolyte in the Mysteries was told that he too has to die, but 'die' here was only meant symbolically. The acolyte has to kill out his lower self, through arduous inner training, before the union with his divine spark could be achieved.

But, Jesus was understood to be a person without any lower self, so if he had undergone an initiatory experience in the Mysteries, he would have had no need to symbolically die, let alone to really die. Yet he underwent the actual experience of death, for the purpose, according to St. Paul and others, of doing something extraordinary, on behalf of humanity, a kind of sacrifice.

We have been looking at Greek texts from the gospel writers and others, about the realm of the dead, and found that it is described as an ocean or sea. But one can ask whether the Jewish world, to which Jesus belonged, also had this way of describing the Underworld. The answer is yes; this was also the view of the Hebrews in Jesus' time, as the Jewish inter-testamental literature shows clearly. For example in the Book of Tobit and the book Sirach and other such texts.

So, if we consider the events of Golgotha involving Christ from the viewpoint of mystical Christians, whether originally from Jewish or Greek background, the general orthodox belief amongst Christians that, Christ arose resurrected out of the Underworld, would be to them a way of saying that he was triumphant over some lower malignant reality, and that this was parallel to the Mystery process, where the acolyte conquered his lower self and became united to a deity.

---

[67] In The Apostolic Fathers, Greek texts and English translations, edit. M. Holmes, Baker Books, Grand Rapids, 1992, p.301.

But the mystical Christian would have also believed, from certain statements in the gospels, that for Jesus to be 'resurrected' some process occurred which in some way assists all humanity to attain to their higher self. For example, esoteric texts from this period, found in the ancient library discovered at Nag Hammadi in Egypt, declare that he had permeated the lower Soul World with a spiritual light. This was probably understood as lighting up a pathway for the souls of the dead to move up to the higher spheres. This idea had huge power and importance to the Hellenistic people because of their own gloomy view on life after death.

In any event, the parallelism between the events on Golgotha hill and that of the Mysteries is now obvious, but it is becoming clear that the events of Golgotha were not a true parallel with these. It was not 'just' an experience of someone being out of the body in a spiritual realm, and then merging with the higher self – colossal though such an experience would be. The early Christians believed that something else, much more potent, took place. Before we look into this, let's sum up the points so far.

Reviewing the discoveries so far

* In the Greco-Latin Age, great sacred sites were no long built, but many lesser temples and communities associated with the Mysteries were established. The sense of the individual self was arising now, as was materialism.

* The crucial events in the new religion of this Greco-Latin Age were crucifixion, a descent into the Underworld, and then resurrection, occurring over three-days.

* But this three-day event is subtly presented in the gospels as a partial parallel to the three-day initiatory process of the Hebrew and Greek Mysteries; it replicated roughly the old initiation process.

* The gospel writers recorded the words of Jesus (Eli, Eli...) in such a way as to indicate that it is connected with the call of the Hierophant in the Mysteries.

* The first literary evidence of a major change in humanity occurs, i.e., a disbelief in things spiritual, and this results in a pronounced fear of death.

* The texts of the new religion actually have two levels, a public level concerning an ethical presentation about the sacred, and a secret level, of relevance to those seeking spiritual rebirth through the Greco-Latin Mysteries.

The promise of aionic (eternal) life

We noted earlier on, that the most important promise or gift that Christ made in his own words, as recorded in the gospels, was that he would give 'eternal life' to people. This point is repeated by St. John, as a primary aspect of Christ, in John 3:16, "For God so loved the world that he gave his one and only Son, that everyone who believes in him may have eternal life."

In today's world, where many people are weary of churches, and often deeply disinterested in spiritual things, this statement seems irrelevant, or at least incomprehensible. But in view of what we so far learnt of the Hellenistic Mysteries, we note here that this promise by Christ is so similar to, but also much more comprehensive than, the offer made by the Hierophants of the Mysteries.

They offered a process that was intended to bestow a kind of eternal consciousness, but to only a selected small number of people. This was a union with the higher self, and with the deity revered in a particular Mystery Centre, such as Demeter. So, what does 'eternal life' actually mean, and how could a human being possibly ever offer to do this?

This expression, in Greek, is zoaen aionion ('ζωὴν αἰώνιον') and in this phrase there is the key word, 'aeon' (αἰών). This word often means multiple cycles of time, but it can also mean 'spiritual realms', despite lack of awareness of this in theological circles. So to make the difference between these two clear, let's say that there can be an 'aeon' or a long period of time, or there can be an 'aion', which means a spiritual realm. The term is everywhere translated as 'eternal' in Biblical texts, however our specialized textual study of how this word is used throughout Hellenistic Greek documents, has shown that this widespread conclusion is incorrect.

For it means very often a spiritual realm, (an aion), and moreover when an epoch of time is meant (an aeon) this is **not** eternity, it is a set time period or a 'time-cycle'. Although occasionally someone in ancient times did incorrectly use aeon (αἰών) to mean eternity, in the same way today people use a word incorrectly. Some scholars have concluded that it is possible for this word to mean a spiritual realm, but this concept is not commonly found in the theological world.

A striking example of this spiritually unaware attitude is found in the translation of a Hellenistic Hebrew mystical text closely associated with the Bible, called 4 Ezra, written probably a few decades after the time the gospels were written. In this text, the word aion (αἰών) occurs a number of times, where it can have the meaning of time-cycles, or Ages, but there are places where it definitely has the other meaning, namely of spiritual realms.

In 4 Ezra, in 9:18, God speaks to the seer Ezra, about his deed of creating humanity, and here the word aion (αἰών) occurs, but here it clearly refers to a spiritual, transcendental realm, and not a period of time. (33) In the sentence it actually occurs twice. It is translated by the respected theological scholar, G. H. Box as,

"For there was a time in the eternal Ages when I prepared for those who now exist – before they had come into being – a world wherein they might dwell..." [68]

But here Box is avoiding the much more likely translation of this term, in accordance with accepted practice of omitting reference to esoteric things. He renders it firstly as a questionable term, namely multiple never-ending eras of time, "the eternal Ages", and then in its second occurrence he translated it as "world", which in fact this word can never mean. One cannot have of course, a multiple of 'eternal Ages'; eternity can only be a single, infinite never-ending thing. So the sentence actually has no meaning in this version. In terms of Greek usage of the key term here it should be translated as follows,

"For there was an occasion in the Aion (spiritual realm) when there was prepared by me, for those who now exist – before they were created – an Aion in which they may have abode {in the future}...." [69]

---

[68] 4 Ezra, trans. G. H. Box, The Apocrypha and Pseudepigrapha of the Old Testament, OUP, Oxford, 1979.

[69] From the Greek text, ʹοτι ἐν καιρῷ ἦν του αἰωνός, ἑτοιμαζότος μου νῦν τοῖς οὖσι πρίν ἦν γένεσθαι αἰῶνα ἐν ῳ κατοίκεν ...

90

Here the sentence reveals that its origin is in initiatory knowledge, and it takes on a high meaning, namely that God, from within a spiritual realm, undertook to prepare a spiritual habitation for humanity. Perhaps this means at some future time, after the Earth has ceased to exist, when humanity moves up to the non-material state of being. In any event, the term 'aion' here does have this meaning of a spiritual realm.

We cannot go into a more detailed study of this word in Hellenistic literature, but such a study shows that when Christ says, in John 6:40 and elsewhere, that he gives 'eternal life' or 'zoaen aionion', he is actually saying that he will bestow consciousness (or life, that is, ongoing existence) in the aions, which means in the realms of spirit, after death.
But this is precisely that goal for which the acolyte in the Mysteries in all Ages was yearning !

And none more so than those living in the Greco-Latin Age, gripped by their fear of death. Once this understanding arose for the early mystical Christians, it is no wonder that they felt a holy awe about the central figure of this new religion. But for other people with some initiatory knowledge, who did not see the veiled textual message, people like Porphyry, Celsus, and Emperor Julian the Apostate, the claims of the new religion seemed exaggerated.

Finally, we need to consider briefly a subject which really needs an entire book – namely, why did the early Christians actually accept Jesus' claim of granting consciousness or life in the aions, the spiritual realms. Why did these early Christians feel that a man, a human being, could make such a claim? We know that for the majority of sincere Christian people, the teachings of Christ, and his miracles, were a major reason for believing his words.

But, it is unlikely that those few Christians who had earlier been initiated in the Mysteries would have accepted this statement without some further special knowledge. People like Clement of Alexandria, who were very aware of esoteric ideas, would not have been fully convinced, without some additional factor. They would have felt that such a deed as granting an aionic consciousness to all people after death, really had to involve a deity, not only a person.

But as the new religion developed, it became humanistic in its piety, not mystical-esoteric. It became remote from esoteric ideas; a condition that worsened as the Greek texts were translated into Latin, and eventually the Greek was known only a few scholars. This process caused the New Testament to lose these hidden spiritual meanings, as these were of course hidden in the Greek, and could not be transferred into another language, especially since the translators had no idea by then that these meanings were even there!

A striking example of the loss of a sense for the multi-aspected spiritual amongst the theologians, is seen in the famous core phrase, 'the kingdom of heaven'. There is in fact no such phrase in the Greek text ! Jesus always says, 'the kingdom of **the Heavens**'. However, humanistic Christianity regards this reference to a multiple of heavens as a left-over from an old Jewish 'superstitious idea', which Jesus utilizes, in order to 'speak their language'.

It never occurs to church authorities, that such an explanation is highly suspect. The very idea of a great religious teacher using an incorrect term for divine spirit reality, in order to keep in line with some current, but false, popular view is hardly valid. And since we know that St. Paul taught that he arose up to the third heaven, this explanation is obviously inconsistent with their own texts.

The Messiah: a human or a god?
It was a core theme in the Mysteries that to give such a priceless gift as that of extended higher spiritual consciousness, a deity had to be involved, and even then the gift of this deity was only bestowed upon an individual acolyte. Hence the cry of the hierophant at Eleusis to Brimo Demeter, the great Earth-Goddess, affirms that she had assisted the acolyte to achieve a union with his or her higher self. Clement of Alexandria was a deeply pious Christian; and yet he obviously felt that it was a valid statement that Christ had an immense power, capable of changing how people existed in the Hereafter.

So, let's return now to our question, why did such mystically oriented early Christians accept this claim from Jesus, when Hellenistic initiates would have been puzzled or outraged by it? The answer lies in a remarkable approach to the central figure of Christianity. An approach which was no doubt very widespread throughout the Christian world in the Greco-Latin

Age, but which was rejected in the 4th century, and banned a century or so later.

This view concerns the nature of the Saviour, whose name was Jesus, but who was given the title 'Christ'. He is regarded theologically in mainstream churches as a mysterious and sacred mixture of human and divine elements. However the actual nature of this mixture, its proportions and dynamics, prior to the birth of Jesus, and afterwards, but especially after the Baptism in the Jordan, is very unclear. Even if it is defined formally in official dogmas, the definitions themselves are not precise, and one sees that exact definitions about complex transcendent topics are simply not possible for the church.

By the 5th century AD, the theme as to whether the Saviour was divine or human, and in what way, became the subject of intense debates in the church. Indeed these debates could and did lead to the murder of those who held opposing views, under the general topic of Monophysitism. But we don't want to examine these debates here. However in the first few centuries of the Christian era, there once was a very different view, and this is expressed in a commentary written by the great Christian thinker Origenes of Alexandria (185-254 AD).

Origenes was a genuinely pious, saintly man, with profound insights into Christianity. Earlier in his life he had studied under both Clement and Ammonius Saccas, one of the really great neo-Platonists. So he could approach Christianity with the mindset of a person familiar with the Mysteries.[70] In his commentary on the gospel of St. John, written in Greek, there is a remarkable passage where he speaks about the nature of Christ. So what is this idea about Christ as a cosmic being?

---

[70] He wrote possibly as many as 600 theological treatises, but a lot of Origenes' writings did not survive the destructive campaign against him, by the church authorities, which broke out two centuries or so after his death.

Chapter Eight: The sun god and heresy

A sun god Saviour: words of Origenes about a cosmic Christ

To understand this passage, one has to know that in the Hellenistic Mysteries, there was an understanding that there were many spiritual realms, and these were the habitations of many kinds of spiritual beings. This view was also shared by some people in the early years of Christianity; they referred to these beings, as the 'divine hierarchies'. This belief did not contradict the monotheism of the Bible, because these great beings were regarded as vessels of God's will. So, the monotheism was not undermined, as these other beings served the one, greater Being.

The text by Origenes here (and many of his texts) appears to be an abbreviated version of what he originally wrote, probably made by someone else at a later time. Unfortunately, the three translations available in English or French over the past 200 years, have failed to convey the actual meaning of this passage; so this striking idea has not been discussed in theological circles. (See the Appendix for more about these earlier translations.)

Origenes is speaking of the cosmic, supra-human aspect of Christ, which is referred to today by modern mystical Christians as 'the cosmic Christ'. This includes, but is not limited to, a great spiritual being called the Logos, who is emphasized in St. John's Gospel, and who is also mentioned in Greek Gnostic texts. Now at this point we need to know that the ancient Greeks could refer to many kinds of spiritual energies resounding through the cosmos to the inner ear of these seers, as 'a logos', or in plural as various 'logoi'. But in these usages, it simply means a resonance; whereas in St. John's Gospel, and with an initiate like Heraclitos, the word 'logos' refers to a real being.

To understand the passage from Origenes, we need to note that in his writings the more-than-human aspect of Christ has **two aspects to it, or rather, consists of two separate beings, who are closely interlinked.** There is a being called the Logos, a very lofty spiritual reality, filled with wisdom and who is part of a primal Trinity. The Logos mentioned in St. John's Gospel is a high spiritual being who created everything. This Logos aspect is mentioned in a letter by St. Paul in Colossians 1:16,

> "For by him all things were created: things in heaven and on earth, visible and invisible, whether thrones or

powers or rulers or authorities; all things were created by him and for him."

But in addition there is also, according to Origenes, a lesser, yet still very high being, from among the ranks of 'the hierarchies', who are better known as the 'mighty hosts of heaven'. The early view of two kinds of cosmic beings, each of whom is called confusingly "Christ", is obviously much more complex than what we now know as Christian theology! The somewhat awkward version of Origenes' text confusingly refers to both these aspects of Christ as a Logos. The idea of two beings who are referred to as Christ (and also as a 'logos') is simply unheard of in modern theological circles. But it was known to the earlier initiatory Christians.

In his commentary on the Gospel of St. John, Origenes has been writing about the Logos, whom he understood as the primal wisdom of God, because he believes that this Logos entity is inspired from sublime wisdom of God. Then he starts to explain that Christ **in his second aspect**, is a particularly high spirit being who is associated with a group of powerful spiritual beings, although not as high as the Logos. These are the famous divine hierarchies of Hellenistic mystics.

So here is the passage from Origenes, I have added some explanatory words where necessary,

> And further, for the clear understanding of {the second, lesser aspect of) the   Logos-{Christ} having its own defined, separate-being, of the kind attaining life of itself, one must speak also about mighty spirit hosts, not only Might. *"For thus says 'the Lord of the mighty Spirit-hosts'* is frequently set forth in Scripture, {and this phrase} means certain spiritual Intelligences,   divine, living-beings;   referred to as "mighty Spirit hosts" – of whom the highest and finest was Christ. Christ, who is designated not only the Wisdom of God {primal Logos}, but also the Might of God {hierarchical being}. [71]

There are nine ranks of hierarchical beings, but a mystical Christian in ancient times could refer to the finest spiritual being in each of these nine ranks as "Christ"; that is, as a kind

---

[71] Origenes: ΩΡΙΓΕΝΟΥΣ ΤΩΝ ΕΙΣ ΤΟ ΚΑΤΑ ΙΩΑΝΝΗΝ ΕΥΑΓΓΕΛΙΟΝ ΕΞΗΓΗΤΙΚΩΝ, in Sources Chrétiennes Origène Les Éditions du Cerf, Paris, 1996, Tome 1, 208.

of vessel of the great Logos. Just as other mystics refer to all beings as a manifestation of God. These ranks of spiritual beings are: Angels, Archangels, Principalities, Powers, Mights, Dominions, Thrones, Cherubim and Seraphim.

Having written this extraordinary passage, saying that the hierarchical Christ is unique in that he is the highest of his particular rank of beings, Origenes continues on, teaching that the primal sublime Logos (the World-Soul of Heraclitos) is also unique, in being truly a sublime and definite entity, not just one of the many vague cosmic resonances,

> "**Just as** therefore numerous mighty Spirit-Hosts of God exist, each one of whom has individualization, (yet amongst all of these is the Saviour, who is higher than the others), **so too** even if the Logos is not individualized anywhere outside us - he the Christ {the Logos} will be understood through the elucidations in previous pages as having real being, in the beginning, in Wisdom." (34)

When we examine both these paragraphs, we discover that Origenes is saying that each of these two Christ beings has a unique quality. Firstly, with regard to the hierarchical Christ, from amidst the "mighty hosts of God", this being is actually different, in so far as he is the highest of all of that rank of beings. And so too with the primordial Logos, although this being is not individualized in the way that hierarchical spirits are, it is not one of countless impersonal cosmic resonances (logoi), for already in the primordial beginning the Logos did possess a kind of real being-ness, and indeed it was in fact divine wisdom itself.

So Origenes taught then, that the cosmic aspect of Christ can not only be called the 'wisdom of God', when the primordial Logos aspect is meant, but also the 'Power of God' when the other, the hierarchical aspect, is meant. Here we have a truly remarkable statement from a revered and learned church father – that 'Christ' is a transcendent, spirit being, indeed there are two aspects to his divine nature, namely the highest of these powerful spirit hosts as well as the primal logos, close to the ineffable Father God. And so all of this tells us that by implication, Jesus is a man, namely that man who became the vessel of these divine beings.[72]

Origenes is in effect saying that the Saviour of the Christian religion is a man, but there is, apart from the man Jesus, a separate spirit being called Christ. Indeed two separate beings of this name, each with their own especial greatness. So is this the answer? Is this belief in a (twofold) cosmic aspect to Christ the actual reason why earlier mystical Christians believed that Christ – understood as two divine beings closely integrated and not a human being – could indeed promise to grant 'eternal life' to all humanity? Just as a lesser god in the Mysteries could grant higher consciousness to the individual acolyte. Logically viewed, this is very likely the answer; and this conclusion corresponds to the teaching of Rudolf Steiner on the subject.

But the question can still arise, is Origenes at all representative of the early Christians, or is he just someone who 'missed the boat' and fell into an unwholesome heresy ? If he is right, then what kind of spirit beings are these 'mighty spirit hosts'? A more radical question then arises. Was this hierarchical Christ being also identified with the great sun-spirit worshipped in Heliopolis in Egypt, and related to Apollo, who was revered in the Grecian Mysteries?

In the Gospel of St. Luke and in the Gospel of St. John there are in fact some striking passages that appear to refer to a deity, and in fact a sun god. The Greek texts of this new religion seem to discreetly present their Saviour as a divine being who is associated with the sun; a being who merged with Jesus at the baptism in the Jordan. There are a number of potent statements recorded of Jesus (i.e., of Christ) in the gospels; statements that appear to transcend what a human can claim to be.

One of these is where he declares that he is "the light of the world". When the original Greek is studied with an awareness of this undercurrent of esoteric wisdom, some statements in John's gospel appears to identify him as a spiritual being, and not a human being. But certainly linked to Jesus. Of course today this would be seen as totally at odds with Christian theology. But the translations which I give here of New Testament passages, from a meditative research into these

---

[72] The man and the spiritual being(s) became merged through the Baptism in the Jordan (another complex subject which we will only note here, but explained in detail by Rudolf Steiner, see the *Rudolf Steiner Handbook*.

texts, are entirely correct, academically, to the grammar of the language. But it is still quite possible for modern interpreters to see my translations as technically entirely possible interpretations, but which have no support from any authoritative Christian source. However, there is very substantial evidence of the early Christians having the same viewpoint as I give here, and this same evidence also shows that this cosmic, esoteric perspective was regarded as secret, as something which was not to be publicly written about.

The sun god descends: heresy or original view?

In the Gospel of St. John, 9:5 an episode is reported wherein Christ heals a man born blind. In the normal translations, Christ says here,

> While I am in the world, I am the light of the world."

But this standard version is not necessarily correct to the original text, grammatically. The word 'while' does not correspond to the Greek word used here, which is hotan (ὅταν). This word means, in this grammatical context, 'many times'. That is, this word means, 'every time that it happens that such and such is occurring.' Therefore, Jesus (i.e., the deity Christ, through Jesus) actually says here,

> "Every time that it is the case that I'm in the world, I'm the world's light." [73]

This sentence is understood in theological circles, using the word 'while', as a statement that declares that the ethics of all good people derive in some way from Christ. Hence on that one occasion when he was living it the world, he gave ethical light to people. But St. John, is more likely saying that each time "Christ" is visible in the world, this same being is a source of illumination for the planet and its ambient environment. It is of course the sun that recurringly provides this illumination for the planet, each morning. This indication that it is not Jesus but actually the cosmic Christ, a being who derives from the sun, who is meant, takes on more substance when one notes the context of this remarkable declaration.

---

[73] Or, one may say, as the Grk. is ambiguous here, "a light to the world", or "the light of the world".

He is about to heal a man who was born blind – thus, someone has never seen the sunlight. But when this man can see, then he will see in fact the sunlight, because the things we see are only seen because sunlight is reflected off them. Sight is the capacity to perceive reflected sunlight. As Jesus prepares to anoint the eyes of the blind man, he refers directly to the sun, for reasons that are not explained convincingly in any theological studies. He says that he must carry out this healing miracle before night-time comes, that is, before the sun has set:

> Jn 9:4 "I must do the work of him who sent me, while it is daytime. Night is coming, when no one can work. Each time it is the case that I'm in the world, I'm the world's light." [74]

These strange words may indeed be seen as a distinct allusion to the sun, because when the sun is in the world (in the sky), it is daytime, but when it has sunk below the horizon, it is no longer a source of light for the world. And this solar allusion is even more obvious when we recall that the Greek word here for 'whenever' actual means that it will be a recurring phenomenon, as we noted above.

So, this sentence is about the many times light comes and disappears ! So, it again appears that the gospel writer wants to suggest that Christ, through Jesus, is saying that he (or rather, It) is the sun ! This possibility is further affirmed by the implication that the healing of the blindness cannot occur during the night time; for the sun's rays are needed.

It is also interesting in this connection that ancient mystical traditions conclude that the power of sight (and the formation of the eye in the embryo) derives from the activity of subtle life-energies which ray into the atmosphere from the sunlight; hence the eye is regarded as a 'solar' organ. For example, Plato wrote that "the eye is by far the most like the sun {of all our organs}, and the power which the eye possesses is a sort of effluence which is dispensed by the sun..." [75] This concept was taken up by a Neo-Platonist, called Plotinus, who wrote, " Never did the eye see the sun unless it had first become sun-like..."[76]

---

[74] Some manuscripts have 'I' whilst others have 'we'. The textual authority in the ancient manuscripts is equal for both versions. It is my conclusion, from the context, that "I" is more correct "we".

[75] Plato: the Republic, sect. 508, trans. B. Jowett, Barnes & Noble, New York, 2004; and Plotinus, Ennead 1, Sixth tractate: Beauty; trans. Stephen MacKenna and B. Page.

[76] Plotinus The Enneads, No. 2, sixth tractate: beauty:

It is significant to note here that the mystic who wrote the Odes of Solomon states discreetly in Ode 15 that 'his Lord' is the Sun. He goes on to say that from the rays of this sun he has been able to arise spiritually, and that his eyes derive from the sun:

> Just as the sun is a joy for those who are yearning for his day, so too, is the Lord my joy. For he is my sun, and his rays have raised me up; and his light has dispelled all darkness from my face. Through him I have acquired eyes, and have seen his holy day...

This statement is referring to the sun as a spiritual entity, or what Rudolf Steiner terms 'the spiritual sun'. The words of the Ode are very guarded, in the customary manner in antiquity of very carefully making initiatory statements which could end up in the public domain. It could mean that his physical eyes were created by the Sun's physical light, or that his soul's 'eyes' were formed from the spiritual sun, so that now he sees more clearly (clairvoyantly). In view of the other mystical statements in these Odes which we noted earlier, it seems to be drawing on the commonly held view (in esoteric circles) that the sun created our eyes, and so the poet is saying his new 'soul-eyes'[77] were created from the rays of the spiritual-sun.

In any event, this association of the Christ with the sun, not only by Origenes, but also by gospel writers, means that these people identified the god of their new religion with the Egyptian sun god, Osiris-Ra, and with the Zoroastrian god, Ahura Mazdao. We noted earlier that the highest deity in most ancient religions was the sun spirit (while the planetary spirits have a lesser rank, in such holistic systems). Hence to the ancients, this leading Spirit of the Cosmos (meaning our solar system) was, in the first instance at least, God. So we may conclude that a form of cosmopolitan religiosity was present in the first phase of Christianity, whose deity was the great sun-spirit. But also, within the sun-spirit-Christ is active the great Logos, part of the sublime Godhead, who transcends the nine ranks of such beings.

Now, back to the writings of Origenes. Some pages before he mentions 'the Lord of the mighty spirit hosts', he comments on

---

http://www.ccel.org/ccel/plotinus/enneads.ii.vi.html
[77] A soul-eye is like the third eye of Buddha; the word chakra comes to mind here.

this healing of the blind man, and says that Christ illuminates the soul of the human being, **as though they were illumined by the sun** (just as the physical sun illumines the body), and that this enables such blessed persons to be able to see the other spiritual beings. But he also says that the souls questing for spirituality, are in fact absorbing spiritual (non-physical) light from the spiritual sun. He puts his astounding holistic perspective like this;

> "For those for who "do not take up into themselves the solar rays of the Christ", the apostles and prophets offer some (weaker) illumination".   (!)

Again one could see this as a poetic image, but in view of other statements from Origenes it appears to be literally meant. And this is one reason, no doubt, for the works of Origenes being banned as heretical some centuries after his death; that is, as contrary to inferior established dogmas. But the evidence is right in the gospels that this viewpoint was not a heresy in the deeper sense. Although it was contrary to what the mainstream had decided upon as the 'truth', yet it was fully in accordance with what the gospel writers themselves understood to be the truth.

It is intriguing that writers can sometimes poetically describe the process of becoming more wise and more spiritual as an 'inner illumination' – so would Origenes regard this as an unconscious manifestation in language of what he specifically believed in his esoteric Christianity? It becomes now a serious possibility that there was a cosmic dimension in the earlier initiatory understanding of Christ, **by the gospel writers themselves**, and by theologians such as Origenes.

It appears that with these first Christians, Christ was viewed as the sun spirit, the sun god of antiquity; that is Christ, not the man Jesus. Strange as it seems to us today, as further evidence is examined, this conclusion gets stronger. For example, we saw earlier how Origenes defines Christ as the highest and finest of the spiritual hosts or spirit army of God.

Now, the Hebrew word, for 'God' in the Old Testament, is 'the Elohim'. This word is sometimes used in the Bible in the plural, implying a number of beings, as if the God of the Hebrews is a being, who has a group of beings associated most closely with him. These beings are of the same rank generally, but of lesser greatness, individually. In any event, by medieval times, the various ranks of spiritual hierarchies, known from the Hellenistic Mysteries, had each been allocated a planetary sphere as their domain.

The various ranks of spiritual beings were experienced as having a specific planetary 'sphere' as their field of influence, so to speak. The solar system was regarded as en-souled by hosts of spiritual beings, and each rank of being was experienced as manifesting in a particular planet's energies. And of course, these planetary spheres encircled the Earth, because the old Ptolemaic solar system was used, in which the Earth was in the centre of everything. And those 'mighty spirit hosts' that make up the host of the Elohim, to whom Origenes refers, **were associated with the Sun**. In the language of the Hellenistic mystic, they dwelt in the sun-sphere; they were sun deities.[78]

It is interesting in this connection, that the stem of the word God in Hebrew (El in El-ohim) was a generic term for God throughout the Semitic-Mediterranean peoples, and in at least one of these ethnic groups, the Zabriern, it did specifically mean the highest of the sun gods.[79] So, in John's gospel, and in the writings of Origenes, there are passages which indicate that the cosmic being called Christ is regarded as the highest of the spirits in what the Hellenistic world termed the 'sun sphere', and thus of the sun spirits, or the 'powerful spirit hosts'.

It appears that the understanding behind this is that, just as the sun is the greatest body in the solar system, so too, the highest of the sun deities would have to be the foremost being of our cosmos (i.e., of the solar system).[80] Rudolf Steiner refers to Christ (the sun-god) as the 'cosmos-spirit'. He uses this expression in his great meditative verse, the Foundation Stone meditation, when referring to the Mystery of Golgotha "...at the turning-point of time the light of the Spirit of the Cosmos entered the earthly stream of being..."[81]

So the church father Origenes is saying that Christ was the leading 'spirit of the cosmos' so to speak, and hence one presumes that Origenes understood Christ as a parallel being to

---

[78] So, in this scheme, the Elohim are then the same beings as the Greek sun-sphere deities called, Exousiai (ἐξουσίαι).

[79] J. Fürst, Hebräisches und Chaldäisches Handwörterbuch über das Alte Testament, Vlg. Bernard Tauchnitz, Leipzig, 1863.

[80] The logos is understood as **beyond** the solar system, but presumably was understood to have associated its energies with the Power, or cosmic Christ.

[81] In usual translations it is poorly rendered as, "the Spirit Light of the World".

the Egyptian sun deity, Ra, who is often described as the creator of all. But as we saw earlier, Ra is an agent of an unknowable, ineffable father-god figure, called Atem, and so too in Christian doctrine, Christ is the agent of the primal God.

And thus Horus, the intermediary between the sun god and humanity in the Egyptian religion, was presumably understood by esoteric Christians to be a parallel being to Jesus, who was the vessel of Christ. On this point, it is striking that in the ancient Egyptian after-death rituals, the deceased soul says of Horus,

> "...and Horus has made for me a spiritual body (soul-form) containing his own soul, so that I may take possession of all that belongs to Osiris(-Ra) in the Underworld." [82]

This would parallel the statements of Christ, made as it were, through Jesus, that he gives to humanity an aionic existence, that is, a future existence, with self-awareness, in high spiritual realms. And also that Jesus is the way to the Father God. So it appears that with some early Christians at least, the sacred processes of the Mysteries, about the need to unite with the sun god, were also involved in the 'Mystery' of Golgotha, in which a kind of potent universal process was wrought for humanity by the events during those three-days. This process involved the union of a cosmic Christ reality to the Earth.

It was Rudolf Steiner who brought the most complete and insightful teachings on this subject. In his book *Christianity as Mystical Fact*, and in various lecture cycles, he explained how the descent of the great sun god, the cosmic Christ imbued the Earth with a divine light, from which the planet itself received a renewal of its life-forces,

> ...if millennia ago someone were to observe the Earth over many centuries, from far out in space, with clairvoyance, they would observe the Earth's aura with its manifold colours and forms. In that moment when the blood flowed from the Redeemer they would have seen the entire aura of the planet undergo a tremendous transformation...a radiant golden star arose (and continues to shine brightly) in the Earth. At this moment

---

[82] Egyptian Book of the Dead translated E. A. Wallis-Budge, p.253, p.78.

is the Earth permeated by the forces of the cosmic Christ.[83]

But also very importantly, Steiner taught that human beings who seek spirituality may now absorb from this radiance those spiritual energies which create the spiritual self.

However in the course of time, the concept of the two distinct spirit beings, with a human being as their vessel, and thus the potent deepening of Christianity that this aspect brings, was gradually lost. Awareness of this cosmic aspect to the Christ-event faded away. The question of just what kind of being is the Christian Saviour, then became the subject of intense but confused theological debate, within the constraints of an increasingly non-holistic, anti-Mysteries worldview.

The resulting concept of an intermingled God-man being, is one which has never yielded satisfactory clarity over-all. The implication of the more holistic viewpoint is that at the baptism in the Jordan, a divine being, the 'sun god Christ', the highest of the sun spirits (in whom there is an aspect of the even higher deity, the Logos), descended upon the man Jesus, at which point he became Jesus the Christ.

Today, there is almost no trace left in Christendom of this earlier view such as Origenes declares; it is now defined as the heresy of Adoptianism. So modern theology speaks of 'the birth of Christ' at Christmas, but some of the earlier Christians knew that it was more correct to speak of the birth of Jesus then.
The above document from Origenes is almost the only ancient document presenting this view of Jesus Christ to survive the campaign by western Christianity against such 'heretical' views.

So, in the light of this extract from Origenes, one can conclude that some early Christians regarded the central entity of their religion as a divine spirit being, indeed the highest of the sun spirits, who united to the man Jesus. The reverence for the sun god, and the view that the sun had the highest spiritual reality in our solar system was a conviction of people in the earlier Mysteries from Egypt, and also in the Greek Mysteries and the Persian Mithraic cult, stimulated by the earlier Persian religion of Zarathustra, with its focus on the sun-like deity called Ahura Mazdao.

---

[83] From his lectures of 2nd Dec. 1906 (Cologne), 22nd Nov. 1907 (Basel), and 1st April, 1918 (Berlin).

Now today, many Christians would recoil from all this, and say that this is really a strange Alexandrian theological mistake, rightly rejected by other early church authorities. And indeed the prevailing attitude today about this is, that it is a distortion of the true Christian message, by Alexandrian Christians who were still partly sun worshipping 'pagans'. But, to say that Origenes and St. John himself, the deepest of the four Gospel writers, were wrong in having this same view, is an obviously wrong conclusion, showing that attitudes of today, opposed to Origenes' views, are themselves in error, deeply.

For there is further evidence that evangelists themselves, from their inner link to Jesus Christ, understood 'the Christ' to be the sun spirit. In the original Greek of another Christian text, the Gospel of Luke, there is a powerful passage which also discreetly describes the Saviour of the new religion as a sun god (see below). To unveil this, the new tool for assessment of the Greek New Testament which this author has been developing, is again needed; the Initiatory Critical Analysis tool.

The Initiatory Critical Analysis tool
We will briefly explore a passage in the Christian scriptures about the mission of the Saviour as being involved with a descent into the Underworld, a journey that was called a 'katabasis' in the Mysteries. And of course this is completely along the lines of the procedures undertaken in secret places in the Mysteries. At the beginning of his gospel, St. Luke, freely utilizing texts from the Hebrew Scriptures, gives a veiled indication as to the cosmic aspect of the Christian Messiah.

He quotes from Hebrew Scriptures which prophesy the coming of the 'Messiah' to people existing in darkness. It is a well-known and beautifully poetic passage, but unknown to the majority of Christians, it conceals a profoundly cosmic message. Let's recall here, that it is usual with passages that conceal an initiatory meaning for the Greek text to be convoluted and grammatically difficult. The NIV renders this passage as,

> "Salvation {is coming}...because of the tender mercy of our God, by which the rising sun will come to us from heaven to shine on those living in darkness and in the shadow of death, to guide our feet into the path of peace." (1:78-79)

This lovely passage may be considered simply as a fine piece of figurative speech, as it certainly is in the texts of the Hebrew Scriptures from which it is taken, (Psalm 107:10,14 and Isaiah 9:2; 59:9-10). But it appears that by varying (or deliberately 'misquoting'), the Old Testament text, St. Luke actually intends it to refer also to the dead, and to a mission of the cosmic Christ involving the dead. The accepted translations miss many fine points of grammar, which veil a message which, when perceived, directly reveals a mystical meaning in the text. We shall consider a few extracts, in a less technical manner, from the treatise where this passage is analysed in the way indicated.

Firstly, in the version given above, we read, "the rising sun will come to us from heaven", this gives the reader the impression that this refers to the man Jesus. However this universally common translation is fully grammatically incorrect. Luke carefully **avoids** presenting the rising sun as simply a metaphor of a human Messiah coming to earthly humanity. Rather the text is declaring something, called 'a rising', which brings radiance, shall visit from spiritual heights.[84]

There is, grammatically, no clear reference to a human Messiah here at all. The reason that the personal Messiah is not clearly delineated here, is that the reality who is going to 'visit' the Earth, is not the Messiah or a prophet, rather it is 'a rising'.

Now that is a strange statement, because a 'rising' must be of either the sun or of a star, but not of course, of a person. Further, this 'rising' is described here as a spiritual reality. There is also the implication that it results in an increasing radiance for the Earth when it arrives. Furthermore this radiance comes 'from above', in the sense of having its origin in a spiritual realm. Therefore one can conclude that Luke is referring to a source of spiritual illumination, rather than to a person.

Further, the Greek verb 'to visit' used here means to specifically, dynamically, seek out something to visit, not just casual visiting. So, this means that 'It', the radiance, will be really 'manifesting' or 'appearing' to people who are in a certain situation; it is not just simply passively seen. Now, this same verb is also used in

---

[84] The word used for 'heights' also has this connotation of a high, heavenly world in Ephesians 4:7 and in an ancient non-canonical text known as 1Clement 36:2

this same way in other Greek literature, **especially in regard to the 'appearing' of the god Artemis in the Mysteries!** [85]

Moreover, the verb is also in the 'aorist' tense, which is a grammatical device in Greek, to show that what it refers to is a once-only event, rather than an ongoing, repeated process. So a **unique** event involving a rising radiance is involved. It is now clear that these strange allusions can no longer be simply regarded as a poetic way to describe the advent of the (human) Messiah.

For significantly, the phrase is referring to the appearing of an illumination-bringing 'rising', rather than a person. The impression given by the Greek text is of an illumination that descends from the heights, as if a spiritual 'appearing' to a lower state of existence is meant, suggesting a descending to the level of human consciousness. There is a milieu of darkness implied here; as Professor Meyer comments, it is as if "there shall be the rising of a bright-beaming star of the night" (rather than a person), from a heavenly realm." [86]

The above suggestions become confirmed when these verses are further examined. Firstly, to speak of people existing "in the shadow of death" is a rather melodramatic expression to use for the people of Israel in the first century AD, but, as we have indicated earlier, it is certainly not so for the dead in Sheol. For enforced inactivity, or a state of disempowerment, accords very well to the understanding of the state of the dead in Hellenistic times, as we noted earlier. This is one reason that there was such interest in the Mysteries and their promise of a real existence after death.

Furthermore, the usual translation refers to the people as "living" in the shadow of death, yet it is quite erroneous to translate the Greek word here ('kathaemenois') as 'living ones'. For if Luke had wanted to refer to earthly people living their lives, he would have used the Greek verb zao (ζάω) which means 'to live'. This verb is used almost exclusively in the New Testament for precisely this sense. Or, he could have used the verb katoikeo (κατοικέω) which means 'to reside, to dwell'.

---

[85] Moulton, James and Milligan, George. The Vocabulary Of The Greek Testament illustrated from the Papyri and other non-literary Sources. London: Hodder & Stoughton, 1930.
[86] Critical and exegetical handbook to the gospels of Mark and Luke, H.A.W. Meyer, trans. R. Wallis, Edinburgh, T & T Clark, 1883.

But the verb of the participle 'kathaemenois' used here (κάθνμαι) means primarily to sit; it rarely refers to 'living', and when it does, it implies a very passive sense, indeed conveying the meaning of being useless, or being in a state of dis-empowerment, or living in a particularly sedentary manner. So, the people are not **living** in the shadow of death, they are 'seated' which means they are in a disempowered state. Furthermore the people are in 'skia thanatou' which means, in "death's shadow".

Now this can be viewed as a poetic reference to living people, but in fact the dead are thought of in Hellenistic Jewish traditions as 'shadows'; their realm is called 'the realm of the shadows'. More significantly, in Hellenistic cultures the about-to-depart soul of an aged person, seen somewhat exteriorised about their body, was actually called, a 'shade'. [87]

Furthermore the word for darkness, used here, skotos, also refers to the darkness that exists in oceanic depths, and as we have seen, the Jewish and Hellenistic understanding of the realm of the dead was that, qualitatively, it resembles a deep ocean or a deep sea. The dead languished there in torpor and, further down, below them, evil beings lurked. For example the Book of Job (26:5) speaks of "the dead in deep anguish – those beneath the waters, and {those} that live in them."

Further, king David, when feeling near to death, writing in one of the Psalms, when his words were put into Greek in the Septuagint's translation, uses the same key words as Luke uses here; David writes of God putting him into "the darknesses {of the oceanic Nether-world} and in death's shade". Note here the allusion to dark multiple realms of the disempowered dead.

A full analysis, of which I have given only an extract here, continues on to show that in the gospel itself, the 'Christ' is discreetly presented as a spiritual being of a sun-like radiant nature, and who will undertake a task in the Netherworld, on behalf of the dead. This view of the Golgotha events sees them as events that are the deliberate climax to the three years of the Saviour, who is in effect a vessel of a cosmic being. This viewpoint of Luke also indicates that these events are partly a replication of the usual Mysteries, and partly a more potent process than that.

---

[87] Article "skiav" in 'A Greek-English Lexicon of the New Testament', W. Bauer; trans. W. Arndt & W. Gingrich, 2nd edit, Univ. Chicago, Chicago, 1979, p. 755.

There follows now the correct translation of this passage which confirms that the events on Golgotha hill were understood by the gospel writers as indeed a replication of the initiation process offered in the ancient Egyptian and early Greek mystery centres, but with a more cosmic dimension. When its veiled message in this passage is uncovered, it is proclaiming this:

The sun god descends   St. Luke: 1:78-79

> Salvation {is coming} ...
> through the fervent compassion of our God,
> (*not 'tender' mercy*)
> by which a Dawning-Radiance from the heights of
> Heaven shall make visitation to us,
> (*not 'the dawn' shall simply passively visit*)
> in order to dynamically appear (*hence to give light*)
> to the people in the oceanic Netherworld   darkness
> (*not just physical darkness*)
> and languishing dis-empowered in death's Shade –
> (*i.e., in the shadowy soul-body*)
> in order to guide our feet into the path of peace.

So, already in announcing the birth of the child Jesus, Luke gives a veiled indication as to the future mission of the Saviour or cosmic Christ being, which later occurs at the 'Mystery' enacted at Golgotha. It becomes ever clearer that the New Testament contains a veiled initiatory message. So, here very early in the Gospel of Luke, Christ is viewed as the sun spirit, appearing to the souls of the Dead, although this is a veiled declaration.

What Luke discretely writes here precisely confirms our analysis of a passage in Peter's epistle which we noted earlier, "For this is the reason the gospel was also preached {by Christ whilst on the cross} to dead persons {in Hades}, that they may be judged indeed as to..."

The extraordinary attitude spelled out in Peter's text (1Peter 4:5-6), which we saw earlier, that there is a cosmic dimension to the Golgotha events, and to the new religion's Saviour, was no doubt of huge significance for those esoteric Christians who were aware of the oceanic Underworld. It would also have been of potent significance to those who were interested in the Mysteries of Isis, for example.

This is because something similar was believed about the initiatory experiences that led to an encounter with this goddess. The second century AD novel which we noted earlier, *The Golden Ass*, gives a fairly accurate presentation of the belief in this, with regard to the Mysteries of Isis, for the goddess promises her acolyte that,

> " You shall live in blessedness...and when you have finished your life-course and descend down to the Underworld, even there in that lower realm you shall perceive me, shedding light into the gloom...you (as an initiate) shall inhabit the Elysian fields {heavenly realm}, and shall continually worship me..." [88]

The difference is of course that Isis does not descend to the Earth, and never had a physical human being through whose death she could sacrifice herself. So, some major new aspects to the spiritual quest emerged with this religion, some of which we have noted, many others of great interest cannot be explored here.[89] But we can now conclude that the events of Golgotha replicated the Three-Day initiatory sleep, the descent into the Underworld, the triumphant call of the Hierophant. But it is also a reversal of the usual process, in that the major element of it is that sun spirit has descended, while the acolyte ascending was a minor aspect, in effect.

Before we consider briefly the hidden indications in the New Testament, let's see what evidence there is of a belief in the solar Christ in very early Christian writings. Already in the Book of Malachi, the last book of the Old Testament, the author writes about Israel awaiting the coming of the Messiah, and calls this being "the Sun of Righteousness"; a remarkable phrase to use, considering that any form of worship of celestial deities was forbidden in Judaism.

Similar statements are found in very early Christian texts, for example in Clement of Alexandria, when he writes to non-Christians in his treatise, "Exhortation to non-Christians". At the end of this work (Chapt. 11), he suggests that Christ is the true Helios. Helios is the god who is known in the Greek culture as the sun god, he who is pictured as driving his chariot across the

---

[88] The Golden Ass of Apuleius, trans. W. Adlington, edit. H. Darton, Henri Navarre Society, London, 1924, p.338.
[89] Also why the triumphant cry on the cross (Eli, Eli..) occurs just before the death, and not at the end of this initiatory process is beyond the scope of this book.

sky. Clement when speaking of Christ, takes up the words of Malachi, and then gives Christ a quite distinctive Helios quality, saying that he is,

> ...indeed "the Sun of Righteousness" who drives his chariot over all, traversing across all humanity equally, resembling the Father, who 'causes his sun to rise upon all human beings' and distills the dew of truth..... [90]

And in a similar vein, Clement's student, Origenes, wrote that people who strive spiritually as Christians may receive "the solar rays of Christ"![91] Now this and other such references can of course be viewed as purely poetic phrases; but as we have seen above, the solar nature of the cosmic Christ is an inherent, basic fact of the gospels. But there are also some very early artworks that appear to derive from the view of Christ as a cosmic being, namely, the sun god. One of these is in Italy, in the Vatican necropolis.

The Helios Christ near the Vatican necropolis

A remarkable work of art was found in an ancient tomb some metres underground in the Vatican Necropolis, underneath a Basilica dedicated to St. Peter, so not far from St. Peter's gravesite. The artwork is a mosaic in a tomb dating back to about AD 250; and is called "Christo Sole" (Christ as the sun). See illustration 2 for a view of the mosaic, partly reconstructed and freshened in its colours. This reconstruction allows one to see approximately how it appeared some 1,750 hundred years ago.

It is certainly reminiscent of Helios, yet the charioteer, who is set in a glowing golden scene, cannot be Helios because he holds the Earth in his hand, in the form of a radiantly blue globe! (Various people in antiquity knew that the Earth was round, but this knowledge perished in the Dark Ages). Helios was never described in this way. And also instead of the crown of rays that the Greek deity Helios usually has on his head, the charioteer has an aureole or glowing aura around his head. And from this, rays of energy spread out - roughly anticipating the cross-like rays which were later depicted with images of Christ.

---

[90] ...ὁ γὰρ τὰ πάντα καθιππεύων δικαιοσύνης ἥλιος ἐπ᾽ ἴσης περιπολεῖ τὴν ἀνθρωπότητα τὸν πατέρα καὶ καταψεκάζει τὴν δρόσον τῆς ἀληθειας.
[91] ... τὰς ἡλιακὰς Χριστοῦ ἀκτῖνας ...

And additionally, the outer area of this mosaic is decorated with vividly painted grape vines; this is a symbol which has no connection to Helios at all.

It is however a specifically Christian symbol, and was used in a major parable of Jesus about workers in a vineyard, how the owner of the vineyard was expecting some reasonable return from the use of his land and vines by the laborers. And even more relevant is the reference to grape vines in the striking words of Christ recorded in the Gospel of St. John, 15:1-4,

> I am the true vine, and my Father is the gardener. Remain in me, and I will remain in you. No branch can bear fruit by itself; it must remain in the vine. Neither can you bear fruit unless you remain in me. I am the vine; you are the branches. If a man remains in me and I in him, he will bear much fruit; apart from me you can do nothing.

Finally, the figure also appears to be wearing a beard, a feature never part of the figure of Helios, but associated with Jesus Christ in many artworks. So, just a few decades after Clement, and at the same time as Origenes was writing, this Roman tomb depicts the Christian Saviour as the new sun god ! This strongly suggests that Christians not only in Egypt but also in Rome were aware of the link between Christ and the sun.

Such an expensive tomb, created from great numbers of beautifully made mosaic tiles (tesserae), is unlikely to have been constructed to celebrate Christ in the dress of a pagan god. It is much more likely that the owners were stating that the sun god is Christ, and that Helios was an earlier symbol of this same being.

Another example of a very early artwork depicting Christ as the sun is to be found in the Italian town of Ravenna, not far from Venice. In a museum called the Museo Arcivescovile, there are a number of artifacts that were salvaged from a church built about 350 AD. One of these is a ceramic carving that depicts a face inside the sun with rays, see illustration 4. It now hangs on the wall in this museum, as a mute testimony to a belief in the link of Christ to the sun from Christians who lived in Ravenna about 1,700 years ago. It is a wonderful experience when visiting Ravenna to see this remnant of an ancient, true knowledge.

3 CHRISTO SOLE or Christ as the new sun god, Helios
A mosaic from a tomb made in a. 250 AD in a Vatican necropolis
(partially restored by computer graphics)
Christ with 2 horses and a sun chariot, and holding the globe of
the Earth in his hand.

It is intriguing to note here an incidental statement in a rare Christian document, which suggests an awareness of what the Hellenistic Mysteries understood to be the threefold nature of the sun. This view saw the sun as not only the physical globe, but also as a dwelling place of spiritual beings, and yet also as a source of divine being-ness on a level higher than those other spiritual beings.

This statement is to be found in an old rare Syriac document from the 9th century, found in Persia in the 19th century, written by a saint of the ancient Syrian Nestorian Christian church, called Mar Ephrem. In discussing how the spiritual person will open their soul to the divine, he likes this to opening the door of one's house to the sunlight. He says, "The **visible** sun is equal for everyone also, but if a man does not open his door, it has no opportunity to enter." Nowadays we would never use the adjective 'visible' for the sun, unless we are contrasting it to an invisible sun. This strange usage appears to suggest an **invisible** spiritual sun. [92] (43)

---

[92] Mar Ephrem: in L. Abramowski & A. Goodman, edit./trans. A Nestorian collection of Christological texts, Vol II Cambridge Univ. Press 1972.

Chapter Nine The ascent to divinity in the Mysteries

Union of Earth and Sun

In Egyptian texts about life after death, it is described how the soul rises up to the sphere of Ra, the great Sun-spirit, (often called the Realm of Osiris) and the implication is that the initiation process replicates this, in a lesser way. So, the acolyte in the Egyptian Mysteries, and no doubt in those of other lands, during the initiation process, induced by the three-day sleep, was enabled, after undergoing the descent into the Underworld, to ascend up to the sphere of the Sun (spiritually viewed). The acolyte had to ascend up to this high realm.[93]

But the Egyptian texts also declare that the lesser deity, Horus, the divine hawk, is the intermediary between the striving soul and the sun god Ra (or Osiris, who stands in for Ra in some ways). Horus helped the acolyte reach the yearned-for realm.

Now a significant question arises here, in regard to the cosmic view of the Christ, which Origenes puts forward, and which is also secretly communicated in the gospels. The central being in this religion is thought of as a divine spirit-being from the sun-sphere. And in the miracle of the healing of the blind man, as reported by St. John, it appeared that the sun had to still be above the horizon, as if some kind of subtle solar energies were needed to restore sight.

Then, we saw how, hidden in the gospel account by Luke, at the time of the crucifixion, this being would descend into the Underworld, and ray forth light. But for this to happen, in the mystical view of the first Christians, the cosmic Christ must have descended down from higher realms, into the terrestrial sphere.

The writers of some of the esoteric Christian-Gnostic texts found at Nag Hammadi in Egypt, declare that this is what did happen. And the implication of this is that a permanent change to the 'soul' of the Earth, to its spiritual energies, was brought about.[94] But in Christ descending down to the Earth, this is no longer a replication of the Mysteries, there is something new here, even a reversal of the process undergone in the Mysteries.

---

[93] For a reliable guide to ancient Egyptian initiatory life, see the book The Great Pyramid and the Sphinx, Damien Pryor (Amazon/Book Depository)
[94] For example, in the Trimorphic Protennoia (para. 40); the Gospel of Philip, (para. 70); the Testimony of Truth, (para. 32-33).

4 **Christ as the sun god, Ravenna ca. 350 AD** This carving was saved when the ancient church was rebuilt; currently in the Museo Arcivescovile. A ceramic carving that depicts a face inside the sun with rays.

The "Mystery" of Golgotha is then, that the great sun god did descend into the lower world – namely that of the Earth (its aura) – with all of the dark miasma that has developed from the lower self of humanity over the ages. And somewhat like the acolyte in the Mysteries, this divinity then arose empowered, to become the glorified indwelling spirit of the planet. So, a kind of cosmic parallel to the age-old initiation process occurred. (We shall later explore this idea of the cosmic Christ as the Earth-spirit, further.)

Now there were of course various esoteric groups opposed to the new religion; one reason may have been that they simply found this concept of such a reversal of the long established procedure to be totally unacceptable. It had always been the case that the acolyte rose up in his soul, to the spirit realms, and never that the sun god or some other lesser deity, descended.

Esoteric groups in the Hellenistic Age probably knew the concept of an 'avatar', as it is called in the Orient. This is a person upon whom a higher spirit being has descended. The Jewish high priests knew about the possibility that one day the Messiah would appear on the Earth, as that was part of their religion and its hopes for the future.

It was understood by these priests that at a future time a divinity, an aspect of God (referred to as Jahweh-Elohim) would manifest on the Earth, merged in some way with its human vessel. It may have been just acceptable to them theoretically that this divinity could in fact be the sun god (if they were open to the older idea of locating divinity in the cosmos). But the thought that this had really happened 'before their noses' without them noticing it, and by using someone who died by the dreadful ignominy of being crucified, seemed most unlikely.

However, the Scriptures prophesied the Messiah would appear, and if the divine is present in the Messiah, then he would have to be in effect, a kind of avatar. But for the highest spirit being of the solar sphere to descend down to the Earth, and appear as the Messiah, by overshadowing a person, would have been an extremely strange idea, even for those with a background in the Mysteries. Surely, to a high priest in the ancient Egyptian times who was involved in the initiatory rituals associated with Great Pyramid and other monuments, this very idea would be unthinkable.

It was a reversal of the initiatory process, on a huge cosmic scale, affecting not just one solitary acolyte lying in the sarcophagus, but humanity in general. For the theologian today the idea that the Christ was a deity with a specific link to the spiritual level of the sun is also unacceptable, but not for the same reasons that the Heliopolis priests would have given; theologians don't factor in any specific cosmic aspect to their religion.

The location of divinity

At this point, we need to clear up a source of confusion concerning the so-called 'Sun-Spirit'. It was quite a strange discovery in our exploration of Christianity in this Greco-Latin era, to find that Christ, the central being in this religion, according to its inner initiatory teachings is viewed as the sun spirit. That same divine being who is associated with the sun in other religions. Our encountering of a secret layer of meaning in the grammatical structuring of the Greek texts reveals that the gospel writers themselves did understand the Christ as a being associated with the sun.

Various scholars, including some atheists, have perceived solar nuances in the Christian religion. They often conclude that the Christian religion is a revised version of an old pagan sun-cult, and was created for political purposes. Or that it is a misunderstood re-statement of the ancient Egyptian sun-cult of Osiris and Horus, because of the many striking parallelisms between these two religions.[95]

These conclusions are wrong, as it is clear that the Christ was thought of as the sun god in the earliest Christian documents, (once their hidden message is seen) and that the gospel writers themselves were placing a dual message in their writings. There is a hidden layer, indicating something which they sincerely believed to be the actual situation, the descent of the sun spirit into the human person chosen for this role.

This Hellenistic view seems a ludicrous idea to anyone who is a sincere Christian today, as it appears to be something in which only crude 'sun-worshippers' would be interested. We need to note here that the problem lies in the difference in attitude to the Divine between the ancient religions and modern people. To the ancients, the divine was quite specifically allocated to places

---

[95] A German academic, C.H. A. Drews became famous a century ago for his books that insist that Christianity is only a solar myth.

in the cosmos; the divine was not a nebulous thing, in terms of the structure of the cosmos. We noted earlier how the solar system had its ranks of hierarchies in the planetary spheres. However, as the Greco-Latin age ended, this specific locating of the divine faded out into something quite nebulous.

In the modern religious world, "God" or Christ" can be defined in terms of holiness. But divinity is not at all perceived, or defined, in terms of its location in the universe. Indeed the very concept of a location of a holy being in the cosmos seems odd.

However, to the more holistic consciousness of initiated persons in the Hellenistic world, this was not an odd concept. The difference is simply one of depth of perspective. The leaders of the sacred sites obviously had an holistic view of the sun; they saw it as having several layers of reality.

Yet the modern person is oblivious to all this, and concludes that the concept of a divine sun spirit is something slightly unsavoury, immature or superstitious; 'You become a sun-worshipper, not a Christian". Today a religious person would prefer to acknowledge the Divine (called God or Christ or some other name) as the origin of their own spirit, without any locality being placed onto this being (other than 'Heaven' perhaps).

So, how does one come to an understanding of the reverence of the sun spirit in antiquity, including the first Christians (i.e., those who had an initiatory awareness.) Well, as we noted earlier, modern astronomical science has revealed multiple layers of energy radiating out from the sun creating in effect, various different suns, on an energy level. The initiatory perspective, underlying the reverence of the sun spirits, is saying that there are still other aspects to the sun, beyond mere energy levels. As the sacred sites testify, to earlier peoples the cosmos was en-souled in quite specific ways. Belief in this higher sun reality is indicated in the sphinx at Giza, who represents the sun god Ra, and is called Horus-in-the-Horizon.

The wisdom behind the structure and initiatory purpose of the Great Pyramid itself came from the priesthood at the town of Heliopolis, the sacred site of the sun god. The central importance of the sun in ancient religions is well known, and is shown in the orientation of Stonehenge to the midsummer sunrise, and its alignment to the interplay of energies between the sun and the moon, at its major standstill. The fascinating ancient Celtic site of the Externsteine in northern Germany was also oriented to the mid-summer sunrise.[96]

So the identifying of the Christ with the great sun spirit of the earlier religions is in effect saying that the Messiah is the primary spiritual being of the solar system, and that this divinity has undertaken a descent to the Earth, to assist humankind. This help occurs not only in terms of ethics (via the parables recorded in the gospels) but also in terms of radiating out a spiritual light that helps people to develop a spiritual awareness – both here on the Earth (becoming an illumined person) and therefore also in the Hereafter (not being stranded in the gloomy Sheol-Hades darkness).

Finally, there is a possibility that an unusual mystical text from the early centuries of Christianity conveys this secret initiatory perspective that Christ is viewed as the sun spirit. It is in a letter said to have been written by Dionysos the Areopagite, the notable Greek student of St. Paul, in which he states that he was in Egypt when the Crucifixion took place, and that he saw the strange darkness, which occurred then, as reported by the gospels. What is intriguing here is that Dionysos at that time – prior to his meeting with St. Paul – was a so-called pagan, and he was studying at the sacred site of the Egyptian sun god, Heliopolis. This situation in effect gives support to the solar aspect of Christ from a very prominent ancient sacred city dedicated to the sun-god.

Dionysos and the Christian sun god
We saw earlier that the famous Athenian Christian, Dionysos the Areopagite, is linked to Heliopolis in early Christian writings. It may well be true that he did travel to Heliopolis, and hence it is a possibility that Dionysos learnt from Egyptian priests about spirit beings having their realms in the solar system. But in his seventh letter, he himself (i.e., whoever wrote this document) specifically states that whilst he was in Egypt, he witnessed the strange darkness that occurred when Christ was crucified. This part of the story has an intriguing implication.

To explore this we need to note that in initiatory literature from many cultures, a mystical fact is often concealed in popular stories. This technique was widely used in Hellenistic times; its

_____

[96] See the books by Damien Pryor for more about ancient sacred sites; Stonehenge, Lalibela, the Externsteine and the Great Pyramid and Sphinx.

most common form was in the formulating of myths. According to the gospels, a strange darkness (a dust storm?) is reported to have happened during the Crucifixion of Christ. This is described by Luke as follows:

> It was now about the sixth hour, and darkness came over the whole land until the ninth hour, for the sun stopped shining. And the curtain of the temple was torn in two. From the sixth hour until the ninth hour darkness came over all the land. (chapt. 23: 44-45)

Now, in the seventh letter of Dionysos it is written that he (and a colleague), whilst undertaking their celestial studies at Heliopolis saw this darkness, and noted how unusual it was. Indeed he concluded that it had a supernatural cause. We note here that they were 'pagans', because Christianity at the time of this event did not yet exist. Thomas Aquinas quotes the words of Dionysos from this document, and says,

> When we were together at Heliopolis, we both observed such an interference of the moon with the sun quite unexpectedly, for it was not the season of their conjunction; and then from the ninth hour until evening, beyond the power of nature, continuing in a direct line between us and the sun. And this obscuration we saw begin from the east, and so pass to the extreme of the sun's orb, and again return back the same way, being thus the very reverse of an ordinary eclipse. [97]

Now this is presumably a fictional story; but in its imaginative details we can show how it is really a subtle testimonial from certain Christians, with access to initiatory knowledge, that their Saviour is the sun god. We recall here that with Origenes and the gospels themselves, the event of Golgotha was seen as a descent of Christ into the Earth's interior; on a spiritual level, this means the descent into the Underworld. Now, this account about Dionysos witnessing the darkness descending over the Middle East at the Crucifixion, creates a potent idea in people's minds which links up some really important themes.

That an acolyte of the Egyptian sun god mysteries, (a pagan Greek man who later becomes a famous Christian) witnesses darkness coming upon the Earth at the time of the katabasis of Christ, that is, the descent inside the Earth of that same sun god

---

[97] St. Matthew, Chapt. 27. (*St. Thomas Aquinas and the Summa Theologica* on CD-ROM; Harmony Media, Inc, Gervais, USA.

– and he witnesses this from the sacred site in Egypt of the sun god itself ! So, the reference in the gospel to the mysterious darkness is mentioned to indicate that the New Testament story contains a veiled initiatory message.

What do we make of this legend? To this author it appears that an initiatory message is hidden here, namely as the sun god – he who said he was 'the light of the world' – descends into the Netherworld, darkness envelops the countryside. As the sun god leaves the sky, and descends into the Earth, the sky grows dark. We are being told: it has to go dark because the sun has gone down inside the Earth. And from where did Dionysos witness this event? From that sacred site whose priesthood was responsible for the nurture of the sun mysteries of Egypt, and the design and construction of the Great Pyramid and the sphinx !

The great sun spirit, whose celestial nature and realm was the focus of the ancient Egyptian sun religion, is now being indirectly affirmed in this Christian legend as entering into the terrestrial sphere of things – the home of earthly humanity. Eventually, this legendary account, and all of the writings of Dionysos, were taken up by the mainstream Christian world, without any awareness of its veiled hint about the sun god, of course.

Various pious comments were added to the above account, giving the report a naïve quality, very typical of hagiographical texts. For example, in the Eastern Church the faithful are told that Dionysos, upon seeing the mysterious darkness, said to his friend, "Either the Creator of all the world now suffers, or the visible world is coming to an end." This is obviously a pious fabrication in which the underlying initiatory message is, typically, not seen.

But despite such accretions, this text may well preserve in this story an indication that a sector of early Christianity believed that their Saviour was a cosmic solar deity. See the Appendix for more about Dionysian Writings.

Key points

* The promise of new religion was the gift of 'eternal life', which means specifically, to retain a conscious existence in the after-death state: an 'aionic consciousness'.

* But to achieve an 'aionic consciousness' was the great hope of those initiated in the Mysteries.

* The gospels indicate that this gift of an 'aionic consciousness' was achieved through the events on Golgotha hill, but was not a personal event.

* Some leading early church fathers viewed Christ as a deity, associated with the Sun, and Jesus as a man. Thus substantial numbers of Christians in the early church must have been in agreement with this.

* Some words of Christ in the gospels indicate in a veiled way a link between Christ and the sun, on a spiritual level.

* The Mysteries teachings were that an acolyte ascends up to the deity, during the three-day sleep, who bestowed a new consciousness on the re-born acolyte, by exerting an influence in the soul of the person. In the Egyptian system, the deity was in what the Hellenistic mystics called the Sun-sphere.

* Jesus the human 'vessel' of Christ, offers a similar influence in the soul by some new sacred process, which does not require the three-day sleep procedure.

* The Greek gospel texts of the new religion, and the esoteric gospels found in Egypt, imply that the deity of this religion, i.e., its cosmic being (Christ), descended down to the Earth.

* Early Christian authorities (Origenes) regarded Christ as a deity, a sun god.

* St. Luke presents in veiled language the initiatory doctrine of the Saviour as a sun god descending to Earth.

Hostility to the Mysteries triumphs
In 330 AD the balance of power between competing religions changed when a brutal Roman emperor, Constantine the Great, decided to integrate the new religion of Christianity into the political-religious fabric of the empire, as part of his political ambitions. He had moved his court to Constantinople, thus generating a new era, later referred to as the Byzantium era. Within a few decades of the Emperor's actions, priests of the Christian religion had succeeded in gaining the Emperor's full

support, and then brought about the persecution of rival popular religions or cults such as of Mithra, Isis, etc. Then the age-old Mystery Centres of Greece were closed down by order of the new state-church, Christianity.

However, it is also true that some of these Mysteries were decadent, and were now exerting a sinister influence. It is also the case that more and more people were adopting a humanistic attitude to life, and no longer supportive of the transcendent ideas of any religion or cult. However the profoundly compassionate ethics in the message of the new religion resonated with the marginalized and disempowered groups in the Roman Empire. The way it treated both women and men as equal, and regarded all classes in society, including slaves, as equals, appealed to a deep sense of personal value. It also caused great unease in the Roman Empire, as this could undermine the economy of their society, which was based, at least partly, on slave labour.

Political events unfolding in the fourth century AD meant that the scene was set for a triumph of this new religion over the Mysteries. Christianity's senior figures (its church fathers) had, at best, an indifference towards the initiatory quest. The secret initiatory process inside Christianity would have been confined to a small numbers of senior figures and their students. In 313 AD the Emperor Constantine declared full toleration of Christianity, and was thereafter known as Constantine the First (the first Christian Emperor). This was a relief to those being persecuted, but it was an ill omen for the new religion because, although it brought the persecution to an end, it opened up the way for the church to metamorphose into a military and political power structure, alien to its real spiritual nature.

The majority of Church officials, unaware of the initiatory element of Christianity that could offer a path towards inter-faith dialogue, were now in a position to carry out their political ambitions with the full force of the Roman authorities. These people held a more banal view of Christian spirituality, and hence no doubt had been deemed unsuitable for induction into the new Christian initiatory process. So, neither the concept of initiation, as in the old system of the three-day sleep, nor some new Christian version, had any meaning to these theologians, and hence their antagonism to 'pagan' Mysteries. Eventually, this also meant an antagonism towards the more holistic Christian truths themselves, was inevitable.

The new Christian initiatory process would have presumably integrated new dynamics developed from an understanding of events on Golgotha. But the details of this are unknown to us today, except that it contained seven stages of initiation. As we noted earlier, this is communicated in the letter written by Clement of Alexandria, about a secret Gospel of Mark. But as those church officials who gained the ear of the Emperor were not part of such a process, they consequently had no hesitation in waging a war against the remaining centres of the Mysteries, rather than engaging in dialogue and persuasion. Consequently, sacred sites throughout the Mediterranean area were attacked and the temple priesthoods forbidden to continue their activity.

The activity against the Mysteries now gathered pace. In AD 392 the sacred site of Eleusis was closed down by the decree of the Emperor Theodosius. In AD 529 the Emperor Justinian decreed the closure of the Neo-Platonic Academy of Athens, and of the Isis temple on the Island of Philae in the Nile. As the Byzantium Empire collapsed, Christianity, now devoid of any esoteric initiatory core, became a fully 'western' religion, based in Rome, after the seat of imperial power was transferred there away from Constantinople. The Roman church, now a political-military state power, used primarily a Latin translation of the Bible (Latin being the language of the Roman Empire), thereby destroying any chance of the deeper message, veiled within the Greek tests, from being perceived.

During the Greco-Latin era the Mysteries died out, and in this period a new religion which acknowledged no initiatory core arose, and eventually became one with the State. Yet the deeds of Jesus, and of Christ, were portrayed in a veiled way in the Greek scriptures as a replication of the primary initiatory process of the Mysteries, with one important exception, for both a reversal and a cosmic process affecting the entire Earth was implied. Modern western theology does not have a focus on these esoteric aspects.

But we have been discovering that Christianity originally was a religion that arose as something that has a link to the Mysteries of the Greco-Latin Age, or those of ancient Egypt. Its veiled teachings have a general compatibility with these older truths, as well as new and unique teachings. It has an initiatory aspect which the gospels discreetly declare, this involves a spiritual event which brought about a permanent symbiotic link between humanity, (both the living and the dead), and the Earth, to the central deity of the ancient Mysteries, the so-called sun spirit.

As the centuries passed by, Greek civilization declined, becoming a vassal of the Roman Empire, and then the Christian Roman Empire itself crumbles. There will be no more great Mystery centres. Sacred sites to serve the Christian religion will be built during the Middle Ages, but if they are to remain unharmed, they need tacit or specific permission from the all-powerful Church-State. They will not have an intention behind their design to provide secret chambers for the three-day sleep process and for cosmic experiences. Except that is, for one sacred site, built in far away Ethiopia.[98]

But there is one major theme we still need to explore. We have noted the deeper cosmic aspect to the events of Golgotha, placed secretly in the New Testament. We have also noted that Rudolf Steiner knew of these deep spiritual mysteries and made it a central theme of his Christology that this cosmic divinity united with the Earth, becoming its indwelling spirit, so to speak. But is there any evidence for this in the New Testament?

The Last Supper in John, verse 13:18
In fact Rudolf Steiner insisted that there is, and he often referred to a sentence in St. John's gospel in this regard. From the research we have considered so far, the important idea emerges that the gospel writers themselves, and prominent early Church fathers and various other Christians, considered that the 'Christ' refers to a cosmic deity, a deity associated with the sun. This concept has no theological support today, and indeed has not had for many hundreds of years. But amongst the mystical groups and societies in the western world, Rudolf Steiner is a representative of this idea in recent times. He offered a very different interpretation of the nature of Jesus Christ and the purpose of the sacrifice upon Golgotha hill, which Christians refer to as the Crucifixion and Resurrection of Christ.

As we have seen, Steiner emphasized that the word 'Christ' refers to a cosmic or divine being, whereas the word 'Jesus' refers to a human being, although an immensely holy person. In his view of Christianity, the cosmic Christ is a central element and his teachings are the most profound available on this theme. It is central to his view that the cosmic Christ united to the Earth (to its aura or soul) at the time of the Crucifixion of Christ.

---

[98] See the book, The Lalibela Handbook, by D. Pryor, for more about this remarkable place.

Christ as united to the Earth as well as to the human soul
Rudolf Steiner often taught that the Earth became the body of Christ. To offer some Biblical evidence for this, he would quote a verse from the Gospel for St. John. He explained that this verse provide affirmation, if not precisely proof, of his teaching on this theme. The verse used by him is John 13: 18, and in English translations of his lectures one finds him quoting this verse in this way,

> "Those who eat my bread, tread on me with their feet".
> (45)

In the German text this quote, found in the Luther Bible is,

> „Der mein Brot isset, der tritt mich mit Füßen."
> "Whoever who eats my bread tramples on me."

For decades this verse has been referred to by anthroposophists (the followers of Rudolf Steiner) whenever the occasion required that this cosmic perspective on Christianity be affirmed or defended. But as from the 1990's it became obvious that the sectarian, that is, non-critiqued, usage of this sentence is not a help to disseminating the cosmic view of Christ as taught by Rudolf Steiner. Firstly, the English anthroposophical translation of this verse is incorrect to the German of Luther, which says, "whoever who eats my bread **tramples** on me".

That is one problem, but also for those people representing Steiner, it is an embarrassment that the anthroposophical English version of this verse is not to be found in any English Bible. A great problem here for the English-speaking anthroposophists is that this quote does not exist in any standard English. Nor is it found in any German Bible, except the Luther Bible!

He who shares my bread has lifted up his heel against me
How does this Biblical passage read in standard English Bibles? It reads as follows in the New International Version, (the NIV) as follows,

> "I am not referring to all of you; I know those I have chosen. But this is to fulfill the scripture: 'He who shares my bread has lifted up his heel against me.'

127

Bible translations of the Greek of St. John into English or German are based on knowledge of the fact that the words here in St. John's Gospel allude to a sentence in Psalm 41: 9. Virtually all Bibles in fact stay closer to the Greek than does Luther in his version. The sentence in **Psalm 41** itself in the Old Testament in any standard Bible is usually translated as follows,

> Even my close friend, whom I trusted, he who shared my bread, has lifted up his heel against me.
> Der mit mir das Brot ißt, hat seine Ferse wider mich aufgehoben. (In the German Elberfeld Bible)

The expression, "...has lifted up his heel against me" is an esoteric phrase which clearly states, as a surface meaning, that someone has become an opponent of yourself. We shall consider later just what this strange Hebrew phrase really means. The usual translations of the sentence in St. John's Gospel retain this strange phrase. Thus in the New International Version (NIV) the passage from the gospel (John. 13:18) reads, as we have noted, has the expression, 'He who eats my bread has lifted up his heel against me.'"

It is this sentence that is our main concern. We need to be quite clear about the impact of any change made to this phrase by a translator such as Luther. For the actual context in the gospel is clearly communicating that Jesus is about to pass a sop to Judas who is thereby being identified by Jesus as the traitor, who has become his enemy. But, as we noted above, in the Luther translation the second part of this text reads,

> "Even my friend whom I trusted, one who eats my bread, **that one tramples on me**.
> (Auch mein Freund, dem ich vertraute, der mein Brot ißt, **tritt mich mit Füßen.)** (46)

So with Luther, we have gone from a general phrase about someone being an enemy (lifting up their heel), to the more limited (but more understandable) idea of an enemy trampling upon a person. So here already is a change in the text which Luther made, probably because the reference to a 'heel' is puzzling to any reader. But the change becomes much greater in the translating of this Luther version into English, when given in English-language anthroposophical books. It becomes,

> "Those who eat my bread, tread on me with their feet".
> (45)

The Martin Luther translation

So here a second major problem arises with the use of this sentence in anthroposophical literature. In English versions of Rudolf Steiner's words, the verse is given a widely different meaning from the Luther German interpretation; and the Luther version is widely different to the Greek, in fact it is in fact incorrect to the Greek. To understand these problems, it is important to note that the phrase 'tramples on me' in German is literally 'treads me underfoot'. But this still means to trample upon someone, in hostility. A literal rendering 'treads me underfoot', could only be used so long as one realizes that it does still mean an action of ill-will !

Otherwise one is dissecting an idiom! To dissect an idiom and then apply its meaning in literal terms is usually a ridiculous thing to do. For example the English idiom, 'he is speaking through his hat', or, 'he is a shingle short' can never be presented in their literal meaning. Likewise a German exclamatory idiom, "O, du grüne Nonne" (Oh, thou green nun") has no specific meaning at all. So, the German idiom, 'treads me underfoot' means to trample upon someone, and nothing else. In other words this sentence, in Luther's translation still means that Judas, from ill-will, tramples upon Jesus.

Obviously the translation in English anthroposophical books of this sentence in the Luther Bible, quoted by Rudolf Steiner, metamorphoses the phrase into a fully harmless activity of people just walking around. For Rudolf Steiner recommends doing exactly this, to dismantle the idiom so it becomes thereby a harmless statement. And all this effort appears to be quite incorrect to the original Greek. Hence the rejection of Rudolf Steiner's interpretation of Christianity, by experts in Christian theology. So which one of these two versions is correct? Is it the harmless version of Rudolf Steiner, "tread on me with their feet" or is it the normal Luther meaning, "tramples on me"; which Rudolf Steiner then interprets as a kind of harmless activity?

To theological scholars of Biblical Greek, neither the Luther version nor anthroposophical understanding of it is correct to the text in St. John's Gospel.

Indeed in recent decades a prominent clergyman of the church established with advice from Rudolf Steiner, announced in an official Steiner publication, that Rudolf Steiner had made a mistake, as the sentence simply cannot be translated so as to give it the meaning that Steiner gives it (!) [99]

We note here that the interpretation of Luther is not correct to the Hebrew idiom upon which St. John has drawn. Hence therefore the usage made of it by Rudolf Steiner seems to be wrong. Because the old Hebrew phrase in the Psalm is about an **over-all hostility**, not a specific kicking or trampling action. So, any version that talks about someone using their feet to do something, is incorrect, **whether** it is a harmless walking on something, or an ill-willed trampling of someone. So what is going here? Where will we find any evidence in the New Testament of a great being, the cosmic sun-god Christ, uniting to the Earth?

The sentence can be explored through meditation and also studied with an inner sense for the initiatory wisdom that was inspired into the Greek text by the Saviour, as the evangelist wrote his words. But this requires a study of the Hebrew text from it was taken and the Septuagint or Greek version of the Old Testament, and the Greek of the gospel. If this is done, the following hidden meaning emerges in the spiritual or intuitive part of the soul, and this can be shown to be correct to the Greek,

> **"The one who is consuming living plant foods** ....
> **is eating that which belongs to me;**
> **and those same persons are walking**
> **across me."** (*across the surface of the Earth, which shall soon become my body.*)

The above meaning is not guessed at, nor imposed on to the Greek, but is actually there, hidden inside the very subtle grammar used in this sentence.

In the Appendix I shall explore this sentence in detail and demonstrate how this inspired meaning is concealed within the Greek. The Appendix is a very demanding part of this book, but to discover a cosmic truth of such extensive significance and sacredness existing secretly as a gospel truth is not attained easily. The Appendix will also validate Rudolf Steiner's usage of

---

[99] The priest is Friedrich Scmidt-Hieber, writing in the journal, Das Goetheanum Wochenschrift, 2008, N.24/08.

the sentence in St. John's gospel as evidence of a cosmic being uniting to the Earth, spiritually.

Conclusion:
In this book we have seen that in the ancient Hellenistic world there were the Mysteries which offered an opportunity for acolytes to enter into spiritual world and awaken their spiritual potential. We noted how Homer had written about the initiatory path in his Odyssey, but that this is often not discerned.

We saw that a major aspect of the Mysteries allowed acolytes, after some training, to go through a three-day sleep condition which enabled them to experience spiritual realms where they could encounter their deity. When this was over, they would arise, as if resurrected, crying out how they were glorified by the spiritual transformation they had undergone. This is a process hinted at in the Bible in the incident of Jonah and the whale. It was this experience which gave them a capacity to function as conscious persons in realms beyond the physical temporal state. This was like receiving the gift of eternal, that is, aeonic existence, or in Biblical terms 'eternal life'.

We saw too how the gift of 'eternal life' is the foremost promise to humanity made by Christ, and that this directly spoke to the people of the times, who were the first to testify to a fear of death. We saw also that, hidden in the New Testament are indications that 'Christ' refers to a deity from what is called the 'sun-sphere', whilst 'Jesus' refers to a human being.

We especially noted that in the gospels, the events on Golgotha where Jesus was crucified and resurrected, were written up in such a way as to include hidden references to the initiation process of the Mysteries.

It was taught by Rudolf Steiner that the 'Mystery' of Golgotha however, was not actually the same as a personal experience in the Mysteries. For it was something much greater, in that it involved the descent of a cosmic 'Christ' deity down to the Earth, rather than the ascent of a person up to heavenly realms.[100]

---

[100] It is on the basis of the above esoteric, deeper experience of the Christ-reality that Rudolf Steiner endeavoured to teach people that a new cycle of festivals could be inaugurated. In these festivals the life-processes of each hemisphere, from season to season, would be celebrated and contemplated in such a way as to assist the community to sense how the cosmic Christ-being

The reason that the Golgotha events are so significant is that they brought about the union of this divine cosmic being to the Earth. And this opened the way to spirituality for all who are interested, and this meant the end of the old way of initiation, using the three-day sleep process.

These discoveries provide some understanding of Steiner's teachings that, behind Christianity is a cosmic process, which is more profound in its significance than religion as such.

---

guides and nurtures the various spiritual beings who sustain the cycle of the year, in either hemisphere. For a detailed explanation of this theme, see my book, "Living a Spiritual Year: seasonal festivals in northern and southern hemispheres".

Appendix

More about Dionysos the Areopagite and his texts

We note that there is very little historical support for identifying this first century saint as the author of the mystical writings known under his name. Indeed the weight of the evidence is very strongly on the side of those who regard them as deriving from the 5th century. But yet it could still be the case that the core teachings derive from the first century. Rudolf Steiner taught that these teachings do derive originally from the first century AD. The assessing of texts from esoteric mystical circles is difficult, as it was a tradition in such circles to transmit their treasured wisdom in an oral form for centuries, only committing them to a written form much later. This produces two distortions to the assessment of the text. Firstly at the time the material is finally written down, the linguistic idiom of that century would naturally be used.

And secondly, during the centuries that it was orally transmitted, there may well be some absorption of semantics and of concepts from the various eras through which it passed. Since he was a student of St. Paul, who, as we noted earlier, had initiatory experiences of the multiple heavens, and of the ranks of spiritual beings, it is possible that Dionysos was given a body of initiatory knowledge about these transcendent themes, which he and his successors handed down in oral form for some generations, and which later was partially merged with Neo-Platonic ideas.

Appendix: the cosmic Christ as the Earth spirit?

In this more difficult section, we are now going to explore in detail the sentence in St. John's gospel 13:18,

> "I am not referring to all of you; I know those I have chosen. But this is to fulfill the scripture: 'He who shares my bread has lifted up his heel against me.'

The very pointed question here is, **how can Rudolf Steiner actually use this sentence as evidence for his assertion that a cosmic Christ being united to the Earth? Whether in Luther's version or in any version?** To find this hidden meaning, we need to go back to the old Hebrew text of the Psalm. We shall discover that in the Hebrew Old Testament, Psalm 41:9 contains a complex, subtle Hebrew idiomatic phrase, which however simply reads, in most translations,

> Even my close friend, whom I trusted, he who shared my bread, **has lifted up his heel** against me.

What the original Hebrew phrase means
But these translations are not quite accurate. For what does this Hebrew text in Psalm 41; 9 actually say? It says, mysteriously, when correctly translated, in an expression found only here in the Old Testament,

> "....**my friend**....**he** has *made-great* a heel against me."
> (author's trans.)
> Gam ish shelovmi asher batachi vov ovchel lachmi
> **higdil alai akev**.   (the Hebrew, transliterated)
> (גַּם־אִישׁ־שְׁלוֹמִי אֲשֶׁר־בָּטַחְתִּי בוֹ אוֹכֵל לַחְמִי הִגְדִּיל עָלַי עָקֵב:)
> (the original Hebrew)

A strange expression indeed! The verb used here for '*made-great*' is gadal (גָּדַל), and it means to **magnify, exalt, to increase in power**. And it is used in a negative sense here in Psalm 41. **It is understood to mean that someone hostilely increases their potential to impact on another person.**[101] (He

---

[101] Hebräisches und Chaldäisches Handwörterbuch über das Alte Testament, Dr. Julius Fürst, Verlag von Bernhard Tauchnitz, Leipzig 1863 and Gesenius's *Hebrew and Chaldee Lexicon to the Old Testament*, trans. S. P. Tregelles, S. Bagster & and Sons, London, 1857.

has 'magnified it'.) This same verb is also found in a negative usage in Psalm 35:26 but without the use of 'heel'.[102] In non-esoteric circles it is generally understood to mean, that someone has magnified, or enhanced in a threatening way, their potential to harm you.[103]

So, it is not actually saying that someone has literally 'lifted up his heel' ! It is actually about the over-all lower self of someone becoming stronger against you. The true meaning of the unusual Hebrew idiom was recognized by the translators of the Hebrew Scriptures in about 300 BC when they produced the famous Septuagint. This is a Greek version of the Hebrew Scriptures for Greek-speaking Jews. For in the Septuagint version this sentence in the psalm, when put into Greek about 300 BC reads, in my translation of the passage,

> "The one eating my foods {with me}, he has **exalted** himself against me **with craftiness.**"[104]
> (translated A. Anderson)
> ho esthioen artous mou, emegalunen epi eme pternismon
> (ὁ ἐσθίων ἄρτους μου **ἐμεγάλυνεν** ἐπ' ἐμὲ
> **πτερνισμόν** .) [105]

It is not about a physical heel being lifted up. But in fact the term 'craftiness' used here (pternismon) was actually created from the word for 'heel'. And thus this sentence really means in its underlying structure, something like, 'he has exalted himself against me in a '*heel-ish* way! So the Septuagint still preserves, although in a weaker subtle way, the reference to 'heel'. The word 'heel' is still understood as a symbol of the lower self, and not as a real part of the foot. What is important here is to note that that the phrase, "has lifted up his heel" should read, 'has made great his heel against me'.

So the Luther version is incorrect, and likewise the Steiner English version is incorrect – so far as normal expertise in the New Testament is concerned – because the Greek words used by St. John retain, in a weak way, the original strange Hebrew

---

[102] Namely, '...they magnify themselves against me'
[103] This unique expression is highly esoteric, with other complex meanings we cannot elucidate here.
[104] Septuaginta id est Vetus Testamentus Graece iuxta LXX interpretes; edidit, Alfred Rahlfs, Privilegierte Würtembergische Bibelanstalt, Stuttgart, no date.
[105] From Psalm 40: 10 in the Septuagint, which has a slightly different numbering sequence of the Psalms to that of the Old Testament.

image, namely that a person's over-all lower self, (symbolized as a heel), has been intensified against someone,

> The one eating my bread has lifted up against me his heel.
>
> Ho trogoen mou ton artov epaeren ep' eme taev pternan autou
>
> (ὁ τρώγων μου τὸν ἄρτον ἐπῆρεν ἐπ" ἐμὲ τὴν πτέρναν αὐτοῦ.)

The alteration made by St. John

However let's note right here that the text from St. John's Gospel in the original Greek is actually a slightly weaker form of the Hebrew, for St. John says, "has lifted up", he does not say, "*made-great*" (a heel against me). Yet the Hebrew does **not** actually suggest a <u>trampling</u> of an enemy. If that were the meaning which St. John had in mind, then his text would just say quite clearly, and straightforwardly, that 'Judas has trampled on me'. Instead he uses the old Psalm 41 imagery, although in a slightly weakened form, which indeed does allow perhaps for some broader interpretation, but not so broad as trampling.

In any event, no matter that St. John's Gospel has a weakened version of the Hebrew phrase in the Psalm, this verse in John 13:18, is naturally understood around the Christian world to mean that Judas has become antagonistic to Jesus.   So consequently, in all usual English and German translations of John 13:18, Christ says in effect, in allusion to the Psalm, that his enemy has heightened his hostility, and this is poetically described as 'raising up his heel'.

> "{Judas whom I trusted,} He who eats my bread {right now, the sop}, has lifted up his heel against me."

However in the Luther Bible, the German readers are told that Christ is saying, in an allusion to the same Psalmic text, that his enemy has heightened his hostility, but this is then described in the narrow sense of trampling upon him. The idea of trampling arises with Luther because the word 'feet' replaces the correct word, 'heel',

> "He {Judas whom I trusted,} who eats my bread {right now, the sop}, is trampling on me (treads on me with his feet)."

This Luther translation is not correct to the Greek. Now leaving aside these fine points, the enigma here is that Rudolf Steiner is suggesting that this is not a sentence about a hostile trampling at all ! He implies that it is about a harmless walking-around activity. So the English-language versions of Steiner's words help Rudolf Steiner by using this harmless version. But since Luther here is less correct than other translations, shouldn't his version have been ignored by Rudolf Steiner, instead of being emphasized? We shall discover that Rudolf Steiner's interpretation that this refers to the cosmic Christ becoming the indwelling spirit of the Earth is quite correct.

Rudolf Steiner's use of Luther
The question of how Rudolf Steiner could use this sentence in Luther's version, as evidence that Christ is referring to people walking around on the Earth which has become the vessel for Christ, is certainly in need of an answer. Members of the anthroposophical society and its associated church attempted in the 1990's to do this, but were unsuccessful. The question is acute, given that Luther's version is a less accurate version of the words given in St. John as compared to any other Bibles in German or English.

And furthermore, St. John's words in Greek are themselves an altered version, a weaker version, of the original Hebrew! How can Rudolf Steiner then interpret this sentence as accurate and indeed as something positive, by saying that it has nothing to do with an attack by Judas?

It is one reason why many well-informed Christians, especially leading scholars in the various churches, do not find Rudolf Steiner's teachings on Christianity convincing. There are quite a number of enigmas are here, and for many readers no doubt this has been a cause of considerable disquiet. We now know that the phrase as originally given in the Old Testament, should read, when put into the Gospels, (unless there is esoteric reason to change it), 'he has made great his heel against me', and not "he has lifted up his heel". But in fact in his version of the Old Testament, Luther also translated Psalm 41 in this same way,

> "Even my friend, whom I trusted, the one who ate my bread, **tramples on me.**"
> „Auch mein Freund, dem ich mich vertrauete, der mein Brot aß, *tritt mich unter die Füße.*"

(literally, '*treads me under the feet*'.)   Psalm 41

Compare this again with the normal English versions,

> Even my close friend, whom I trusted, he who shared my bread, **has magnified his heel** against me.

So Luther has weakened the esoteric meaning of this unusual Hebrew phrase in the Old Testament, because he has removed the reference to a heel. He narrowed it down to an act of metaphorically trampling on someone. Luther then uses his narrower view of this complex Hebrew idiom when translating the Greek of St. John. But as we shall see later, his less accurate version is actually a fortunate error.

Like everyone else, Luther thought that one could regard Judas's actions, as described by St. John, to be hostile because it is directly alluding to Psalm 41, and of course since it is about Judas's betrayal, it must be about hostility. Perhaps Luther thought that the original old Hebrew text really did mean attacking someone with one's feet. Luther's translation of this passage suffers from ignoring the underlying meaning of the Hebrew idiom about 'raising the heel', and provides only a narrow version of its true meaning, which is, "The one who eats my bread has strengthened his evil intentions against me".

But this simple clarification about the difference between the standard Bibles' version and the Luther version only brings clarity to the elementary meaning here, about Judas and his political actions. The above explanation, so far, does seem to imply that Rudolf Steiner's interpretation is wrong, that it is less accurate than the standard interpretation in most Bibles. But we have laid the groundwork for actually getting to the solution.

It is quite clear that we have not yet resolved the enigma of how such a sentence can be understood to be referring to the incorporation of the cosmic Christ into the Earth's soul. It appears quite undeniable that, since the Hebrew psalm is about an attack on David, and the Gospel account at the Last Supper is about an attack on Jesus, then the 'lifting up of the feet', or the heel, also has to mean **to attack** someone. It seems to be a reference to the man Judas, not to all of humanity – and especially not in some **positive** way. So just how can this text be seen by Rudolf Steiner as referring to something positive; and also to something which refers to all humanity?

To justify Rudolf Steiner's viewpoint, one has to find a way of understanding the Greek text which no longer refers to either the negative nuance of the sentence as normally understood, nor the specific historical reference to Judas being hostile to Jesus Christ. The grammar has to also allow a **positive** walking activity, not an ill-will trampling. Quite a task! We shall now explore further, without the reader needing an advanced knowledge of ancient Greek.

Secrets hidden in the Greek script

As we proceed, it will be necessary that we note a few points about this wonderful ancient language. Firstly we need to remind ourselves that this passage is of course, about eating, and it is also about the imminent death of Jesus. However, the verb used by St. John in the phrase, 'eats my bread' is the word troegein (τρώγειν) which in fact **is not the normal verb for eating**! To the esoterically perceptive person, this fact is very significant. The usual verbs for eating are either esthiein (ἐσθίειν) or phagein (φαγεῖν). And that is why, when the Septuagint was written, the translators used the normal Greek verb, esthiein.

So it is very significant that some 350 years later, St. John specifically rejected this usual verb and used instead a very strange verb. Secondly, although St. John does indeed use the usual verb phagein quite often for the general act of eating, he uses 'troegein' only five times. But each time it refers solely to the very potent and very esoteric idea of **humanity somehow consuming (that is, absorbing) Christ.** This usage is to be found in chapter 6,

> ^{Jn 6:56} Whoever eats my flesh and drinks my blood remains in me, and I in him.
> ^{Jn 6:57} Just as the living Father sent me and I live because of the Father, so the one who feeds on me will live because of me.

So the first thing the meditant learns is that the usage of this special verb in our sentence (13:18) is intended to direct the meditant's attention to the sacred theme of the inner absorption (or 'consuming') of Christ. And this of course must mean, absorbing spiritual energies from Christ; a cosmic kind of Christ; such an idea just cannot be referring to a human being ! However, considering the cosmic quality of this Gospel, starting as it does with a contemplation on a great cosmic being, namely the Logos, that is not surprising. This also means that a cosmic meaning might very well be hidden in this sentence.

So the usage of this special verb in the sentence in 13:18 is intended to direct the meditant's attention to the theme of the inner absorption or 'consuming' of Christ; that is, spiritually absorbing spiritual energies from Christ ! This is itself a very sacred and potent idea.[106] But this same verb also has two other special nuances. When used of eating by ancient Greek writers in the general sense, it points specifically to the process of really setting out to eat something; of really going through the process of taking nutrient into oneself **actively**, such as by chewing or biting off a portion of the foodstuff.

For example, when it was used of animals eating, it meant the actual process of crunching, chewing or munching, and also then the swallowing. So it would be used in ancient Greek texts, to mean 'the cow was chewing the grass' or 'the horse is biting off a portion of carrot', etc.

Thirdly, we need to note that in an older usage of this verb, it was actually used **only for the eating of plant substances**, that is, fruit and vegetables. It was never used of eating meat. So when used of people, it always referred to eating (chewing and swallowing) vegetables or fruit, and when even used of animals, it referred to herbivores munching, chewing, etc. It never was used to refer to carnivorous animals or humans eating flesh. [107]

We need to note here quite clearly that plant foods are of course an expression of the Earth's life-forces. Plant foods manifest and derive from the Earth's etheric energy-field. Finally, this special verb 'troegein' is a rare word in the New Testament, occurring only six times; it is used five times by St. John and once by St. Matthew.

So the phrase, *"The one 'eating' my bread"* directs the meditative attention of the reader attuned to the Christ mysteries, to people who are actively absorbing, as <u>soul</u> nutrient, through specific inner effort, something that has living energies within it, something associated with the edible plants that manifest the inner life of our planet. In fact, it hints at the

---

[106] This idea or rather deep spiritual truth exists in ancient Egyptian texts about Osiris; a preliminary form of Christ.
[107] Walter Bauer, A Greek-English Lexicon of the New Testament, edit. trans. Arndt & Gingrich, 2nd, edit., University of Chicago, Chicago, 1979 and A Greek-English Lexicon, comp. H.G. Liddell & R. Scott, Clarendon Press, Oxford, 1996.

eating of plants, but plants **as symbols of the Earth's life-forces**.

But it is used by St. John **only in reference to absorbing Christ into one's soul** (absorbing the 'cosmic bread of life'). So here in John 13:18, the 'living thing' or life energies being consumed or absorbed, can only be those life-forces that come from Christ ! And indeed it is Christ who is speaking these words. Bread of course is derived from grain, and the grains are from living plants. The bread is described as belonging to Christ. So Christ here **is directly linking himself to the Earth's life-forces**.

The first thing that emerged from our exploration is a veiled meaning which says, the Earth's life-forces are permeated by Christ. The second teaching now unveiled is, human beings, in eating plant substances, are absorbing Christ. Now before we take the next larger step to discover the next sacred message in this sentence, and thereby discover the deeper meaning of this sentence, we have to know about a special feature of ancient Greek grammar. Let's see the sentence in John 13:18 again, and focus on the next part, about raising the heel. In both the NIV and a non-Luther German version (the Elberfeld version) it reads,

> 'He who shares my bread **has lifted up** his heel against me.'
> Der mit mir das Brot ißt, hat seine Ferse wider mich aufgehoben.
> ho trogon mou ton arton **epaeren** epi eme taen pternan autou
> (ὁ τρώγων μου τὸν ἄρτον ἐπῆρεν ἐπ" ἐμὲ τὴν πτέρναν αὐτοῦ.)

We need to note that the verb used here in the Hebrew original of Psalm 41 ('gadal'), "my friend....he has *made-great* a heel against me" has been put into the imperfect tense, that is, the simple past tense (higdil, הִגְדִּיל). And so following on from this, the Greek version in the Septuagint **also uses** the simple past tense, "...he has exalted himself against me, with craftiness (emegalunen, ἐμεγάλυνεν)."

But in the Gospel of St. John, the Greek verb used here '**has lifted-up**' (epaeren, ἐπῆρεν) **has been specifically put into a remarkable tense or condition, known as the Aorist condition. It is no longer in the simple everyday past tense.** What is the

Aorist condition of a verb?   The word Aorist itself means 'indefinite' in Greek; and this grammatical feature is the key to unveiling the deeper hidden meaning of this sentence, and to thereby discover the core message of esoteric Christianity.

The timeless Aorist condition

This verb condition is not found in any modern language. It is usually defined as being the past tense, especially a one-off past event. In this way this marvellous Greek language can indicate whether an action was ongoing, or a one-off act! For example, if one writes that someone cut down a tree in the past, then the Aorist is used, because that has to be a one-off event. But if a river overflowed its banks, then the simple past tense is used, as this action can re-occur.

But this Aorist state can also signify other things, as we shall see. So the first question arises; why did St. John use here this special condition, the Aorist state?   Why not stay with the simple past tense? It is also very important to note that St. John has thereby **changed** the Hebrew in two ways. Firstly, as we saw earlier, the Hebrew says,"....he has **made-great** ('gadal') a heel against me." but St. John has changed 'made-great' to 'lifted up'. This is the same alteration which Luther made when he translated the Psalm.

When St. John used 'lifted up' instead of a Greek equivalent to the Hebrew verb 'to magnify one's impact', he was doing this very consciously. And yet 'lifting up' is to some extent implied in the Hebrew, because this can be a poetic way of describing from the viewpoint of the observer, the effect when the enhanced potency of someone's hostility is manifested.

So firstly, why did St. John use 'lifting up' and not 'making-great'? And secondly, we must ask the question, why did St. John put this verb into this Aorist condition? The answer to the first question is, the use of 'lifting up' of the heel, (or the foot as Luther has it), rather than 'making-great', **introduces the possibility of the motion of walking**! So we can say at this point, that we have the suggestion of people walking, even if this seems quite accidental, even irrelevant, in the light of our earlier comments.

But we still have the second question, why is the verb in this unusual Aorist condition? If we can answer this, we can discover how Rudolf Steiner could be justified in using this sentence as evidence of Scriptural indications about the cosmic Christ as the spirit for the Earth. But let's just review what we have discovered so far.

Firstly, scholars would say that the Aorist is very often a simple past tense, and so the whole sentence here simply means that Judas, who is eating bread with Jesus, has already planned to betray him. So he has lifted up his heel (or foot) symbolizing hostility, and it is quite clear that it is in the simple past tense, for it is an action that Judas had already planned.

But also we have seen that the sentence discreetly suggests two intriguing things, by the choice of special Greek words; this has not previously noticed by scholars. Namely, that people could somehow be taking up Christ into themselves, as a kind of living nutrient.

Now here we realize something very important has become clear; on this deeper level of meaning, deliberately put into the Gospel by St. John, about absorbing Christ, **actually has to exclude Judas!**

On this level of meaning, about the absorbing of Christ spiritually, the sentence refers to not one individual, but to many people. For it is now about people, lots of people, who are absorbing energies from the cosmic Christ. But is this statement of mine correct? It is actually allowed in the grammar? Yes, it is; for the word, 'the one' (eating my bread....") in Greek, 'ho' (ὁ), can refer to either a single person, or to many people. It is indeed singular, but it can and very often does, refer to many people; it literally says one person but it means numerous people. For example in Luke 6:49 it used in this way,

> The person (in Greek, 'ho') hearing, but not taking action, is like a man who has built a house on the ground without a foundation..."

Here, as in so many other places in the New Testament, this word is singular, but actually implies a lot of people. Some anthroposophists may want to rush in now and say that therefore Rudolf Steiner is right, that the reference to lifting the heel or foot is indeed about walking. But something should still hold such persons back. Namely that negative word at the end of the sentence, 'against'; which implies an attack,

> 'He who shares my bread has lifted up his heel **against** me.'

So are all our earlier discoveries just an illusion? Is the Aorist condition of the verb 'to lift up' simply just another way of putting the past tense here – which it often does in many Greek documents?

Not against, but 'across'
This word 'against' is in fact a preposition in Greek, (epi, ἐπι). But in the Hellenistic Greek language, the meaning that a preposition has in a particular sentence **depends upon its grammatical context**. When used with what is called the dative case, 'epi' does indeed mean 'against'. But here in this sentence it is used with what we call the **accusative case**; and in this context 'epi' almost always means **'across/upon', not 'against'** ! [108] More precisely stated, the word 'epi' in the accusative case can sometimes mean 'against', but only rarely; nearly always it means 'across' (or on, or upon).

If the ancient Greeks wanted to say 'against' by using 'epi' then they would normally use the dative case. For example, of the 476 times that 'epi' occurs in the New Testament in an accusative context, it nearly always means 'upon'. In fact, it only means 'against' in just 30 cases out 476. [109] So this word means primarily 'across', 'on' or 'upon'; depending on the grammatical context ![110] So, now we can take a very significant new step; the last part of the sentence **is far more correctly translated** as, **'*across* me'**, and not '*against* me'.

> 'He who shares my bread has lifted up his heel **across me**.

So now that we know this, we can proceed further. We need to examine briefly the truly remarkable ways in which the Aorist condition of a verb was used. When we do this, we shall discover that it is not limited to the past tense. It has a truly unique quality, a quality which modern languages no longer possess. There are a few sentences in the New Testament where

---

[108] A. T. Robertson, A Grammar of the Greek New Testament in the light of historical research, Broadman Press, Tennessee, 1934 and D. Wallace, Greek Grammar beyond the basics, Zondervan, Grand Rapids, 1996 and A Grammar of New Testament Greek, James H. Moulton, Vol. III, T & T Clark, Edinburgh, 1963.
[109] R. Morgenthaler, Statistik des Neutestamentlichen Wortschatzes, Gotthelf-Vlg, Zürich, 1958.
[110] It is interesting to note that just as the Greek preposition means 'across' or 'upon' (or at times 'against'), the Hebrew preposition in Psalm 41, (**ala-i**, עָלַי), also means 'across' or 'upon' as well as 'against'.

the other, truly unusual meanings of this Aorist condition can be seen.

A past action continued on into the present

Consider this sentence from St. Mark, about how at the baptism in the Jordan, a voice from heaven declared that God was 'well-pleased' with Jesus; that is saying in effect that the divine could be fully manifested in Jesus.

> Mk 1:11 And a voice came from heaven: "You are my Son, whom I love; with you I am well pleased."

Now in fact the verb 'am well-pleased' used here (in all three of the synoptic gospels), is in the Aorist condition, and so it would normally have to mean,

> "You are my Son, whom I love; I <u>was once on one occasion</u>, well pleased with you." (!)

This implies that God is now no longer well-pleased with Jesus, even right now! Quite a problem for translators. They have therefore come to all sorts of different conclusions; but the consensus is that here this Aorist state must have its special timeless quality. So, here it could mean that God was well-pleased with Jesus already in the remote times before Jesus was conceived, and continues to be so now. This would show that Jesus was in unity with God before the world was created. [111]

And it is indeed true that the Aorist condition is simply not always a past tense, even though it accidentally became a kind of past tense. For it is actually about a process becoming completed, any process, but the process can also still be ongoing, right now in the present; it does not have to be only in the past. The Aorist can be used for processes that continuously bring to completion various smaller actions that together create an on-going contemporary process. This is a very strange perspective by our standards! But this is what is going on here in this sentence.

We are told that God has become 'pleased with' Jesus as a one-off completed act (in the past), **and yet this state of union continues on as a completed reality,** and continually renews

---

[111] Ezra. P. Gould, Internat. Critical Commentary; Gospel Mark, T. & T. Clark, Edinburgh, 1897, p. 216 and Joachim Gnilka, EKK, Das Evangelium nach Markus, II/2, Benziger Vlg, Zurich, 1999, p.135.

itself. This we call the gnomic Aorist condition; it is well-known to scholars. So therefore, more correctly translated this sentence reads,

> Mk 1:11 And a voice came from heaven: "You are my Son, whom I love; with you I became well pleased and this is constantly re-affirmed."

So we have discovered that when a verb is in the Aorist condition it can refer to a process which happened long ago, but which is still livingly active in the present. So it ignores the earthly flow of time. The past is viewed as part of the present!

However, the Aorist can also be used in another strange way. It can be used for the reverse of this, for a process which has not yet happened but which is nevertheless regarded as already being a real, living reality in the present! Very strange! Consider another sentence from Scripture. Normally it is translated in the present tense, and yet, amazingly, it is definitely about a future event. This sentence really helps us to understand how sophisticated and subtle is the Greek language. The following is obviously a divine prophecy, and so it is about a future event. It occurs in the description of the Last Supper as written by St. John,

> Jn 13:31 When Judas was gone, Jesus said, "Now the Son of Man is glorified and God is glorified in him."

However the verb here ('glorified') **is twice in the Aorist condition, and so it should actually be translated as the past tense, i.e.,**

> "Now the Son of Man has been glorified and God has been glorified in him."

But this would be absurd, as the Resurrection of Jesus has not yet occurred! So, the normal translations simplify the situation and put it in the present tense. Yet the verb, being Aorist, can be neither in the future nor in the present tense! So here translators usually adopt the compromise of using the present tense in such a way as to suggest the future. Yet the Aorist has **nothing to do** with the present or future tenses at all. So this is baffling, since the future is obviously meant, but just how does the Aorist do this?

The answer is that the aorist condition here is saying that, so utterly certain in the mind of Christ is his prophecy about what shall happen, that it can be regarded as already being completed! So the Aorist is indicating that the process of the Son of Man being glorified shall most assuredly be fully completed soon, and indeed, it is so utterly certain to be completed, that it is presented (through the aorist condition) as an action that has already been completed, with no regard to the flow of time, (for it is still to happen) !

There is no grammatical feature in our language that can do this ! So if one were to try to render the meaning here, it would be a very awkward, very wordy rendering,

> Jn 13:31 When he was gone, Jesus said, "Now indeed the Son of Man shall have already been glorified, and indeed God shall have already been glorified in him. (!!)

Well, this simply is not meaningful to us in any way at all. To us this is simply far too strange a way to deal with the flow of time – something which is definitely to occur in the future is to be regarded as having already been completed. So we actually encounter here a very intriguing grammatical quality of this language; to present as a truth already in the here-and-now something which lies in the future. This is known to scholars as an gnomic Aorist, which means a timeless indefinite condition.

But through a knowledge of spiritual ideas, this situation is actually quite understandable. For where is something already in existence but is not yet manifest in the flow of time? For the ancient Greek people the answer would be, **in the spiritual worlds**! It is there where the past, present and future exist side by side, so to speak. In these realms important truths of the future (and the past) exist as a thought-form. The timeless (gnomic) Aorist is an ancient literary device giving expression to the awareness of spiritual realities that the ancients possessed.

We have seen that the Aorist can be used of an event in the future as if it had already happened, because in the spiritual worlds, in the intentions of the gods, it is a reality, regardless of the flow of earthly time. And secondly, it can used of a process in which actions are continually being completed or past, but the action carries on in the present time. [112]

---

[112] A. T. Robertson and D. Wallace (8) and H.P.V. Nunn, A Short Syntax of New Testament Greek, Cambridge Univ. Press, 1975, p.87 and Samuel Green,

So, the Aorist can also be used to refer to a process whose components recede off into the past, but which also keep repeating themselves as part of a bigger procedure, so the over-all process itself **remains in the present time**. Quite a remarkable grammatical tool ! In Lk 7.35 we find another remarkable example of this,

> NIV But wisdom is proved right by all her children."
> NKJ But wisdom is justified by all her children

The verb here is actually aorist and thus would usually mean something that occurred once in the past, as it does with Luther, who translates,

> But wisdom was proved right by all her children

But it is **aorist** and therefore a gnomic aorist is correct, because a simple past comparison ignores the present and future possibilities, and is thus wrong. So I translate it as follows,

> "Wisdom has been, and repeatedly becomes, justified by all her children."

So here St. Luke is saying that the process of Wisdom (or Sophia) being affirmed through the experience and the actions of sages has occurred in the ancient past, and is also occurring when his text was written, and shall occur in the future.

Spiritual processes via the Aorist in Homer

And in the ancient Classic Greek of Homer, some 800 years before St. John, we find this same kind of suspension of time, and reference to actions which do occur, are completed, but are nevertheless in the present and the future. For example in his great story, The Iliad, in book 16, v 401, where the death of a hero is mentioned, we find,

> haeripe d' hoes hote tis drus   hearipen
> ἤριπε δ᾽ ὣς ὅτε τίς δρῦς ἤριπεν

This is translated by all academic experts something like this,

> ".....and he fell like an oak tree falling."

Handbook to the Grammar of the Greek Testament, The Religious Tract Society, London, 1897, p. 304.

But the verb is in the aorist, and thus it would normally have to read,

> "....and he fell as when an oak tree did once fall."

This is very odd, comparing the death of the fighter with a long past event that once happened, namely when an oak tree fell. But since it is a gnomic aorist, it actually means, when correctly translated, and esoterically understood,

> ".... and he fell, as when every time an oak tree has fallen, or ever shall fall."

From an inner understanding of the text, one can conclude that here Homer as an initiate, is hinting at a Mars activity, as oak trees are associated with the planet Mars. So that, as the martial hero died, Mars forces were released, and these always will be released whenever a strong Mars organism collapses, whether a human fighter or the oak tree, which is traditionally associated with Mars forces. So here again is an action which is completed, but which constantly re-occurs and thus can be considered as being past or completed, yet happening now in the present, and on into the future.

Now, after these examples, let's look again at the sentence that Rudolf Steiner has used as an example of how Scripture points to the union of the cosmic Christ to the Earth, namely,

> "The one eating my bread, he has **lifted-up** his heel *across* me"

Let's recollect at this point that we have already seen that in the lifting up of *the heel* there is a faint reference to people walking. And in Luther, the allusion to walking is much stronger; lifting up *the foot*. And this change was made possible because the verb 'to magnify' was replaced by St. John with the verb 'to lift up'. And we saw that there is also a veiled reference to being nourished, by taking up living plant nourishment. And we noted that plants symbolize the life-forces of our planet. But also we have discovered that the taking up of this living nourishment is about taking up of Christ, since the verb is ever only used by St. John for the absorbing of Christ.

Lifting up the heel or foot
Now here we remind ourselves that the verb 'lifted up' is in the Aorist condition! So, it does not have to be seen as just a simple

past tense. It can also be seen as a timeless process, a continuous completing of **something which nevertheless remains in the present time**. What could that be? Well here that something is – walking! For what do we do when walking? We lift up our heel (or better, foot) and then we place it down onto the ground; but no sooner is this action completed, than we lift up the other foot and complete the next action of lifting up our foot and then putting it down, before starting all over again with the other leg. Walking is a process of **continuously completing the lifting up of the foot or heel**.

Although it is a present action, it contains the past, namely, the continual completing of the process of lifting up the foot! For this type of action the Aorist condition is an ideal device, as we have seen above. So now the esoteric Christian meditant realizes that the sentence is saying here, on this level,

> "The one 'eating' my bread, he is **continually completing the act of lifting-up, and then putting down, his heel** (foot) *across* me."

And in fact this therefore means, when precisely and translated, with spiritual insight,

> "The one 'eating' my bread, he **is walking** *across* me".

Now we need to bring all of this together. The deeper level of meaning can now be seen. For John 13:18 has become a sentence prophesying what shall soon come to pass – but as a direct result of the betrayal by Judas. For what does it now mean to a deeper insight into this sacred Christian text? It now can be seen as conveying the following meaning to the mystical Christians of the first few centuries of Christianity,

> **"The one who is consuming living plant foods** ....
> *digesting nourishment from the Earth's life-forces* –
> **is eating that which belongs to me;**
> *is absorbing Christ's divine life-force in the plants that he sustains,*
> **and those same persons are walking**
> (*continually completing the process of lifting up his heel, and putting it down again.*)
> **across me."**
> *across the surface of the Earth, which has (shall soon) become my body.*

"Those who are consuming living plant foods
are eating that which belongs to me;
and those same persons are walking and those
same persons are walking across me." St. John 13:18

All of this implies that *the Earth is about to become the body of Christ.* The Earth and Christ have become united, and hence people are walking across or upon Christ. This translation is entirely accurate to the Greek, and indeed is much more correct to the subtle nuances of meaning than all the normal versions.

The cosmic Gospel

We have just seen the answer to the question, how can this sentence in the gospel of St. John actually mean what Rudolf Steiner taught. Is there any other evidence that this research here is correct? In the other Gospels the Last Supper includes a very special section; it is the passage where Jesus Christ offers bread and wine to the disciples. The words He speaks there, about the bread being his body and the wine his blood, became the basis for the church's holiest sacrament, the Eucharist or the Mass. The words used then are,

> Mt 26:26 While they were eating, Jesus took bread, gave thanks and broke it, and gave it to his disciples, saying, "Take and eat; this is my body."
> Mt 26:27 Then he took the cup, gave thanks and offered it to them, saying, "Drink from it, all of you.
> Mt 26:28 This is my blood of the covenant, which is poured out for many for the forgiveness of sins.

These words are understood to mean that the individual worshipper may share spiritually in the very being of Jesus. Hence the sacredness of these words. So it is very striking to discover that these words and the associated action of passing around bread and wine, <u>are entirely omitted</u> in the Gospel of St. John! This omission has caused serious difficulties for theologians for many centuries. It seems to be a very serious defect in this Gospel. But once the deeper spiritual message in 13:18 is discovered, then this omission becomes understandable.

Instead of affirming the spiritual union of **individual Christians with Jesus** (and his associated, but undefined, divine-ness), St. John has affirmed, in a veiled way, the initiatory understanding of the spiritual union of the **cosmic Christ** with the **Earth-soul, and through this process with all humanity.** For this reason St.

John omitted the sacramental words from the Last Supper about taking and eating the bread or drinking the wine, because those words are directed to individuals in an ecclesiastical setting, wherein the congregation becomes the 'body', that is a part of the spiritual essence of Jesus Christ.

But this description from St. John is about the larger cosmic perspective wherein all individuals, even if unaware of this, are to become people who, in living on the planet, and so of course walking over it, shall become part of the body of the great cosmic Christ spirit who is to about to become the indwelling spiritual essence of planet Earth. [113] There is therefore an underlying teaching in this sentence, which I would put in this way;

"The Earth has become my body, which is shed for ye."

That is, the Earth has been created to enable humanity to evolve towards the Spirit.

But one last objection could be raised; how can this be the secret deeper meaning of this sentence, because it is spoken **before** Jesus is killed. At the time when this statement is made, it is apparently not true. (!) The answer is that the entire sentence is a spiritual statement of just that kind which the Aorist makes possible. A statement that is above the flow of time. We saw how the Aorist condition for the verb 'to lift up' implies walking, by hinting at a repeated finishing of an action going on continuously in the present.

But as we have also seen, the Aorist enables one to point to events which transcend time, especially if the intention is very important. It points to events or intentions which live as Ideas or thought-forms of the gods. It is quite true that when this sentence was spoken, the union of the cosmic Christ with the Earth **had not taken place.**

But to Christ and esoteric Christians, there is no intention or planned event, formulated by divine beings, greater than the Mystery of Golgotha. It is from the viewpoint of St. John, the very basis for the Earth's future existence. Consequently Christ can indeed proclaim, **before** the event, that He is the spirit of

---

[113] There are references to this cosmic dimension in this Gospel, through the recording of the washing of the feet incident, which has to do with Piscean energies; this matter will be explained in another book.

the Earth, because in this passage from St. John, He is pointing to the imminent occurrence of this supreme event. And to Him, this event is a truth already, for it is an intention in the spirit realms planned by God, and which no power was able to prevent. An intention already planned as in remote ages.[114]

So at the Last Supper, Christ proclaimed it as already a truth spiritually, even though it was not yet embedded in the flow of earthly time. And similarly, as we saw earlier, some short time before this, He had proclaimed the glorification of the Son of Man, even though the event was still to occur in the flow of time. The Aorist condition makes exactly this sort of language possible.

Review
The first level of meaning is historical, and concerns hostility from Judas Iscariot. In the English versions it appears as, **'The one eating my bread, he has lifted-up his heel against me.'** The surface meaning here is that Judas has become antagonistic to Jesus. In the Martin Luther version it appears as, **"He who eats my bread, is trampling on me."** This version means that Judas is regarded as metaphorically trampling on Jesus.

On Level One the above versions are quite correct. Anthroposophical authors have then translated this Luther sentence and made it into something positive, by dismantling the German idiom to trample, and reading it 'to harmlessly walk upon'.

But when a deeper level of meaning in the sacred text is accessed, we see it is hinting that people, in digesting plant foods are in effect absorbing energies from Christ. Because the verb used here means to really digest living (plant-based) food, but yet it is only ever used by St. John of absorbing or receiving into oneself the light of Christ. So it means that people can absorb life-enfilled nourishment from Christ. That points us to the subtle life-forces of the planet, and to the presence of Christ in these. This initiatory or inspired level of meaning in the gospel also then is in harmony with such other words of Christ, as "I am the bread of life".

---

[114] In anthroposophical teachings, this preparation occurred back in what is known as the Sun aeon, see my book, the Rudolf Steiner Handbook, for more about this.

And the people who are doing this, they are all incarnate people, because they are walking along over the Earth. Lastly, human beings, in walking along across the planet, are walking across Christ (not Jesus). John 13:18 is saying that soon people shall be walking over Christ, absorbing the life-forces of the great cosmic god, because He shall soon become the indwelling guiding spirit of the planet.

To point towards this layer of meaning, Rudolf Steiner has used Luther's translation because Luther's German idiom for trampling is literally, "....tread on me with their feet". And by taking this idiom literally one can take a kind of short-cut to the third level of meaning, since it points to people walking along. And this was no doubt an appropriate decision by Rudolf Steiner at the time, and for his purposes.[115]

But it is more secure, and more defensible, outside of German audiences, to take the long route which I have given here. I have attempted to establish the accuracy of Steiner's words, and that the deepest meaning of the sophisticated Greek grammar in John 13:18 accords fully with Rudolf Steiner's explanation, and confirms his understanding of a merging of the deity with the planet,

> "Those persons who are consuming plant foods are absorbing living nourishment from Christ, from within the planet's life-forces, and all such people, in walking over the planet's surface, are walking across Him (for He is to become the indwelling Earth-Spirit)."

And this shall be the case as a direct result of the betrayal by Judas. Christ is shortly to become the indwelling, guiding spirit of the planet. The last meaning is dependent upon the first meaning, upon the death of Jesus, through the Mystery of Golgotha.

****

---

[115] In 1908, Steiner faced a question after a lecture as to why he insisted that this sentence in John 13:18 revealed that a cosmic Christ being would unite to the Earth, when obviously the Greek did not say that. He replied, "Yes it is a shame that this has not been seen correctly, but in the future someone shall appear who shall establish that this sentence does refer to the union of Christ to the Earth." (unpublished Archive document, Frag.-Beantw. #1789)

Some Works Consulted

Novum Testamentum Graece post Eberhard et Erwin Nestle, edit. Kurt Aland.

The Holy Scriptures of the Old Testament; English and Hebrew, The British and Foreign Bible Society, London, no date.

Neues Testament und Psalmen nach der Übersetzung Martin Luthers, Verlag der Canstein'schen Bibel-Anstalt Halle 1870 & Vlg. O. Brandstetter, 1915 Leipzig & Württembergische Bibelanstalt, Stuttgart 1960 & 1980 et al, Deutsche Bibelgesellschaft, Stuttgart, 27. revidierete Auflage 1995.

Maclear, G. F. The Gospel according to St. Mark, Cambridge, Camb. Univ. Press, 1896

Carr, A. The Gospel according to St. Matthew, Cambridge, Camb. Univ. Press, 1894.

Lane, W. The Gospel of St. Mark, NICNT, Eerdmans, Grand Rapids, 1974.

Hagner, D. Matthew 14-28, Word Bib.Comm., Word Books, Dallas, 1995.

Luz, U. Das Evangelium nach Matthäus, 26-28, EKK, Benziger-Patmos Vlg, Düsseldorf, 2002.

Swete, H. The Gospel according to St. Mark, MacMillan & Co, London, 1909.

Buckler, F. "Eli, Eli, Lama Sabachthani?" Amer. Journal Semitic languages & Lit. Vol 55, No.4 pp.378-391 Communio Viatorum, 2, XLIV 2002, Stanislav Segert, The languages of Historical Jesus, Charles Univ. Prague.

McDaniel,Th. Jesus' Last Word in Biblical and extra-biblical traditions – www.palmerseminar.edu/Gospel

Daniélou, Jean. The Theology of Jewish Christianity, trans. Baker, John Darton. Longman & Todd, London, 1964.

Alexandria, Journal of western cosmological traditions, D. Fideler, edit, Phanes Press, Grand Rapids, 1991.

Taylor, Thomas, The Eleusinian & Bacchic Mysteries, 3rd edit, Wizards bookshelf, San Diego, 1987.

Steffen, Uwe. Jona und der Fisch; der Mythos von Tod und Wiedergeburt: www.opus-magnum-de

Hall, M. P. Dionysian Artificers, Macoy Publ. New York, 1936.

Cumont, Franz. The Mysteries of Mithra, Dover , USA, 1956.

Vermasern, M. J, Mithras the secret God, Chatto & Windus, London, 1963.

Davidson, G. A. Dictionary of Angels, The Free Press, New York, 1967.

Plato, Timaeus & Critias, trans. D. Lee, Penguin, London, 1977.

Cornford, F.M. Plato's Theory of Knowledge, RKP, London, 1960.
Albinus, the Platonic Doctrines, trans. J.Reedy, Grand Rapids, Phanes 1991.
Cicero, The Dream of Scipio, trans. P. Bullock, Aquaria press, Wellingborough, 1983.
Plotinus, Enneads IV, trans. A. H. Armstrong, Harvard Univ. Press.
Steiner, Rudolf. From amongst the 360 volumes of Steiner, the reader will find the following books of relevance:
Christianity as Mystical Fact, The Gospel of St. John, The Gospel of St. Matthew.

INDEX

www.ingramcontent.com/pod-product-compliance
Lightning Source LLC
Chambersburg PA
CBHW062044090426
42740CB00016B/3015

* 9 7 8 0 9 9 9 4 1 6 0 2 0 1 *